THE DIVERSITY DIRECTIVE:

Why Some Initiatives Fail & What to Do About It

V. ROBERT HAYLES, PH.D.

ARMIDA M. RUSSELL

**AMERICAN SOCIETY
FOR TRAINING AND
DEVELOPMENT**

McGraw-Hill

New York   San Francisco   Washington, D.C.   Auckland   Bogotá
Caracas   Lisbon   London   Madrid   Mexico City   Milan
Montreal   New Delhi   San Juan   Singapore
Sydney   Tokyo   Toronto

McGraw-Hill

*A Division of The **McGraw·Hill** Companies*

This publication is designed to provide accurate and authoritative information in regard to the subject matter covered. It is sold with the understanding that neither the author nor the publisher is engaged in rendering legal, accounting, or other professional service. If legal advice or other expert assistance is required, the services of a competent professional person should be sought.

From a Declaration of Principles jointly adopted by a Committee of the American Bar Association and a Committee of Publishers.

Library of Congress Cataloging-in-Publication Data

Mendez Russell, Armida.
    The diversity directive: why some initiatives fail & what to do about
        it / Armida Mendez Russell, Robert Hayles.
      p. cm.
    Includes index.
    ISBN 0-7863-0819-2
    1. Diversity in the workplace.   2. Personnel management.
    3. Corporate culture.   I. Hayles, Robert. II. Title.
    HF5549.5.M5M46 1997
    658.3'041—DC20   96–35438

Printed in the United States of America
3 4 5 6 7 8 9 0 DO 3 2 1 0 9 8 7

PREFACE

Background of This Book

Whether the topic was demographic changes, cultural sensitivity at work, or valuing differences among one's colleagues, the 1985–95 decade was a time to jump on the diversity bandwagon. People recognized anew both the interdependence of human beings and the necessity of diversity for organizational survival today. They saw with fresh eyes that the ways people differ lead to either crisis or opportunity: Crisis comes when differences cause conflict and block synergy. Opportunity abounds when differences are combined to create synergy.

So ready or not, organizations of all sorts rushed to implement some type of diversity initiative. Thousands of workers throughout the nation have taken part in one or more days of diversity training.

The most popular initiative was diversity awareness training. Understandably, awareness training focused on individuals, although to be effective diversity work must address organizational systems as well. Reflecting and promoting the individual emphasis, the diversity training and consulting industry expanded dramatically.

As more workers were trained, employers created in-house diversity councils and supported the development of diversity networks linking similar affinity or resource groups across many organizations. The range of perspectives addressed by these networks likewise expanded. From a first concentration on race and gender, the range broadened to issues of culture, age, veterans' status, work life, sexual orientation, disabilities, and more.

The investments made by many organizations in diversity management promised to generate additional benefits beyond those associated with diversity directly. Diversity management efforts frequently led to new organizational systems and structures, as well as entry into new markets. As diversity concepts began to be applied more globally and defined more broadly, they also started adding critical new dimensions to existing organizational initiatives.

Employee reactions to the new initiatives naturally varied widely, too. Often the diversity focus created uncertainty and fear—fear of leveling the playing field and having to share it with previously under-represented groups. Others responded with apathy and annoyance: "Our plate is full already; don't add more to it." But many saw attention to diversity as a chance—at last!—to be heard and included. It changed their expectations for the better.

We've learned a thing or two from these early attempts to create change through diversity. This book builds on those lessons to help translate diversity into visible and measurable results. It is a guide for individuals and organizations to move beyond preliminary initiatives and awareness training toward systems, processes, and behaviors that embody substantive, lasting change. The book emphasizes effectiveness (doing the right things), efficiency (doing them cost effectively and well), and endurance (institutionalizing beneficial changes). The three together make for healthier places to live, learn, and work.

Who Will Benefit from This Book?

The Diversity Directive will benefit anyone working to improve human and organizational performance. It is particularly written for diversity, pluralism, human resource, equity, equal opportunity, affirmative action, and education and training professionals. However, it will be equally useful for proactive workers in diversity change programs—diversity task forces, councils, boards, and audit teams, and the like. There is also helpful material here for individuals involved with diversity networks and employee resource groups.

Many of the concepts, tools, techniques, and models discussed here have been successfully applied throughout the world. They are appropriate—as is this book—for businesses, civic organizations, government agencies, and educational institutions. From them, readers will gain a practical and research-based understanding of diversity work. They will understand how to diagnose individuals and organizations, as well as how to specify appropriate healing actions at each stage of the change process. Additionally, they will be able to point out specific and tangible benefits that flow to individuals and organizations from well-done diversity work.

How to Use This Book

The Diversity Directive can be skimmed quickly by reading the summaries at the end of each chapter. These summaries provide an overview of the whole in one short reading. When more detail is needed, readers can go to the sections of interest within each chapter, as summarized below and further outlined in the Table of Contents. Where necessary, redundancies in the text allow readers to fully comprehend a particular chapter or section without having to refer to earlier sections.

What Each Chapter Offers

Chapter 1: Rationales for Diversity Change
Presents the case for diversity work. Specifies and documents the outcomes and benefits for individuals, groups, and organizations.

Chapter 2: Diversity Defined
Provides state-of-the-art working definitions of diversity from real organizations. Examines key related concepts such as similarities and differences, unity without uniformity, and sameness and fairness. Discusses emerging diversity dimensions.

Chapter 3: Individual and Group Development Models
Primarily for diversity professionals, this chapter presents major individual and group development models that professionals use and delineates their applications. It also offers suggestions for individual and group development processes.

Chapter 4: Organizational Development Models
Another chapter intended primarily for diversity professionals, Chapter 4 presents major models that professionals use, plus a generic summary model. This chapter also includes examples of diagnostic symptoms and recommended treatments.

Chapter 5: Strategy Variations
Presents material to help custom fit a diversity approach to each organization's vision, culture, and needs. Covers issues such as self-sufficiency, top-down versus bottom-up change, pilot projects, behavior change versus attitude change, and general diversity work versus work to address specific issues.

Chapter 6: Preparation: Factors to Consider
Describes important ingredients often overlooked in diversity work. Also addresses obstacles to progress and ways to avoid them.

Chapter 7: The Road to Results
Presents tips for effective implementation, such as linking diversity with organizational objectives and focusing on closing performance gaps. Spells out quantitative and qualitative measures for tracking the diversity change process.

Chapter 8: Conducting a Successful Diversity Audit
Covers all major steps in a good diversity audit, from identifying rationales and winning management support to communicating results and developing action plans.

Chapter 9: The Diversity Change Process, Step by Step
Describes the five major phases in the diversity change process: awareness, transition, adaptation, institutionalization, and alignment.

Chapter 10: Revitalizing Traditional Initiatives
Covers techniques to use when initiatives stall, including enhanced awareness training, employee resource groups, human resource reviews, management practices, and more.

Chapter 11: Diversity Competencies
Explains elements and concepts that support diversity competence. Includes key tasks and skills of diversity professionals and self-evaluation questions.

ACKNOWLEDGMENTS

The authors are indebted to the many colleagues and loved ones who made this work possible. There are too many individuals to attempt a complete listing. If you contributed to the completion of this work and are not mentioned below, please accept our sincere apologies.

Organizational

The Bayer Agriculture Division showed great creativity in applying many of the "how to" tools we describe. The Diversity Council for the Bayer Agriculture Division guided (and continues to guide) that organization's diversity change process using many of the methods described in this book. The Pillsbury Company provided generous support to Robert for research and writing time. Pillsbury also provided a real-world laboratory to test the models and theories described in this book.

Many clients provided application and learning opportunities. Among them are: Allstate, American Express, Ameritech, Amoco, Carlson Companies, Digital Equipment Corporation, Ford Motor Company, Honeywell, IBM, Litton Industries, LTM (South Africa), MIKOS (Norway and Sweden), Monsanto, Morrison Knudsen, Pacific Gas & Electric, Performax PTY, United Way, and YMCA. Other clients included the States of Minnesota, New York, Oklahoma, Oregon, Utah, the Province of Alberta, and the Government of Colombia. Finally, academic clients included Amsterdam Summer University (the Netherlands), Dallas County (Texas) Community College System, Northern Illinois University, and Oakland Community College.

Personal

Armi's family—Lewis Russell, Adrianne, James and Jacqueline Davis, Thais, Andrew and Marcus Lloyd—shared their love and support.

Robert's family—Debra provided intellectual inspiration and substantive contributions. Andrew modeled, like his Grandpa Fuller, an enthusiastic creative approach to life in our diverse world.

Jim Behnke encouraged and inspired Robert to pursue his dreams of writing and consulting, and Lou de Ocejo facilitated the time and focus necessary for him to get it done. Merry Kemp researched definitions of diversity and shared her talents in preparing creative visual materials. Joanne Carlson and Anthony Morley provided excellent editorial support in preparing the manuscript.

Our contacts at Irwin Professional Publishing, Cynthia A. Zigmund and Tracey L. Yeager, were both supportive and flexible. Many colleagues urged us both to write and share our learning.

Romeo McNairy (Ford Motor Company) successfully applied many of the models and tools described in this book. As a talented internal leader of diversity work, he provided many of the examples of excellence cited herein. Special appreciation goes to all those who allowed their work to be cited.

Spiritual

The authors offer thanks for the blessings and gifts from the Creator, who made this book possible.

CONTENTS

Chapter 7

The Road to Results 89

1

Rationales for Diversity Change

Diversity work for individuals involves what we know, how we act, and how we feel—head, hand, and heart. If we focus on any two of these three, the third is consistently likely to follow.

Diversity change begins in the head as we learn more about people who are different from us. It continues as a process of modifying behavior—the "hand"—to become more effective in our interactions with people who reflect different cultures, speak different languages, communicate with different styles, or bring different experiences to their interactions with us. Third, diversity change involves emotional growth in the heart, as we develop authentic relationships with people who are different.

Diversity change also means that as learning and growing individuals we will move through several developmental stages as we confront each significant pluralism issue. The development involves movement from a negative or neutral view of different others to acceptance and respect and, ultimately, to a view that positively values the difference of the person with whom we interact.[1] At that point we grasp group and individual differences without falling into the trap of stereotypes.

Individuals working in organizations where pluralism is effective experience an enhanced quality of life. Taylor Cox sums up the factors that improve performance in a climate that values diversity as "equal-opportunity motivation to contribute."[2] "Equal opportunity" does not mean that benefits are limited to groups usually named in equal-opportunity policies. Everyone shares in a better quality of life when inclusive diversity change takes place. And, as documented later in this chapter, senior managers often find that both their leadership skills and their organizations improve after they engage in personal diversity work.

WHAT DIVERSITY MEANS FOR GROUPS

When groups include diverse perspectives and value that diversity, a number of desirable outcomes occur. Diversity provides immediate access to a larger pool of knowledge, skills, and abilities as the group works to accomplish its goals and objectives. If the climate values pluralism, then synergy is possible. Indeed, synergy is possible *only* when diversity is present and welcomed. Then, differences among individual coworkers can combine to produce positive, documentable outcomes that could not occur if everyone were the same.

The converse is true, too: In the absence of diversity, blunders are likely to occur and opportunities will be missed that a dose of difference in the group could have prevented. News media and marketing literature are full of embarrassing and costly examples, some of which now follow:

- General Motors (GM) had difficulty selling its Nova car in Spanish-speaking countries. "No va" means "no go" in Spanish. Had even one employee who knew Spanish and Spanish culture been present to provide guidance, GM could have saved a great deal of money.
- Non-kosher cheeseburgers served in Israel by McDonald's restaurants caused a fair amount of protest and a large loss of sales.
- The team that marketed Gerber baby food in Africa made the picture on the label a black-skinned baby, yet sales in Africa were very few. Customers there expected labels that pictured the product, not the consumer. Gerber's losses were substantial.[3]

However, there are numerous examples of successes brought about by diversity-smart corporations, as well.

- Kentucky Fried Chicken was successful in Israel with kosher chicken.
- Old El Paso's Mexican product line has been number one in its category for years.
- United Airlines experienced an increase in Spanish-speaking travelers when it installed a Spanish-speaking telephone reservation line.
- Avon Products saw significant revenue growth after it hired African-American, Hispanic-American, and Asian-American sales and marketing professionals.
- The Pillsbury Co. and Kraft-General Foods both reported increased access to African-American and Hispanic-American markets after hiring marketing and related professionals from more diverse backgrounds.[4]

Beyond these numerous news stories and anecdotes is research-based evidence of the benefits brought by diverse perspectives. Diversity professionals now are fortunate to have excellent empirical studies that show the potential and real impacts of diversity on group performance. Here we provide a short review of these findings.

Beginning in the laboratory, research by Harry Triandis at the University of Illinois 30 years ago showed that trained groups representing politically diverse perspectives outperformed equally trained homogeneous groups.[5] Seven years later, Robert C. Ziller reviewed the literature on small-group performance and concluded that diverse groups outperformed homogeneous groups on complex tasks.[6]

Research in the 1980s provided additional empirical evidence. In 1986 Nancy Adler's work on synergy showed that diverse teams are anything but average performers. Adler described several stages of team development, beginning with cultural dominance, moving to compromise, and ending with synergy. Only diverse teams achieved the highest levels of synergy. Additionally, in 1989 *Business Week* reported that investment clubs composed of women and men made more money (10.4 percent gain) than those composed of women only (9.1 percent) or men only (8.7 percent).[7]

In the 1990s, we now find many organizations moving from strictly functional organizational structures to cross-functional teams. Consultants studying the shift to teams informally report productivity gains of 10 to 15 percent as a result of the change. And when cross-functional teams are also demographically diverse, the gains are even larger. For example, Robert Lattimer of Towers Perrin, a consultant based in Atlanta, reported a 21 percent productivity gain from demographically diverse cross-functional teams at General Electric Power Systems against 13 percent from homogeneous teams.[8]

Data supporting the idea that diverse teams are—or at least can be—qualitatively and quantitatively more productive continue to grow as further studies in this area are completed.

WHAT DIVERSITY MEANS FOR ORGANIZATIONS

At the organizational level, most research on the impact of diversity is quantitative. There were no large-scale studies published in the 1970s. The most significant work in the next decade emerged in 1983 in *The Change Masters*, by Rosabeth Moss Kanter. Her work encompassed a large sample of organizations and demonstrated that companies with progressive human resource management (including affirmative action) enjoyed significantly greater profitability during the 20-year period of the study.

In separate works in the late 1980s, Robert C. Levering and Dennis J. Kravetz came to the same conclusion when looking at time frames of five years or longer. Both researchers used indicators such as sales growth, profit growth, and performance in a declining economy.[9]

Thus far the 1990s have included large-scale studies like those of Kanter, Kravetz, and Levering and even some that focus on specific differences. For example, looking only at race and gender, research consultants Heidrick and Struggles, Inc., found that companies with two or more women and two or more "minority" directors on their boards were much more likely than others to be named to *Fortune* magazine's "Most Admired Companies" list.[10] (See Table 1–1.) Similarly, a front-page *Wall Street Journal* article in 1993 reported a study showing that companies with good records of

TABLE 1–1

An Interesting Relationship

	Fortune Most Admired Companies	All-Public Fortune Companies
Have 2 or more women directors	26%	16%
Have 2 or more minority directors	16%	6%

Source: "The New Diversity: Women and Minorities on Corporate Boards," Heidrick & Struggles, Inc., 1993.

TABLE 1–2

Equal Opportunity Pays (1988–1992)

Women and People of Color History	Performance Relative to Overall U.S. Stock Market
In the top 20%	2.4% higher
In the bottom 20%	8.0% lower

Source: The Wall Street Journal, May 4, 1993, p. 1.

recruitment and retention of women and people of color also had stock prices that were about 10 percent higher than those with poor recruitment and retention records.[11] (See Table 1–2.)

In 1994 Robert Hayles, then at The Pillsbury Co., examined the relationship between financial performance and excellence in diversity within the food industry, using a broad and inclusive definition of diversity. First, Hayles rank ordered 10 food companies for financial performance. The indicators used to determine rank were earnings per share, earnings per share growth, and total return to investors during the period under study.

To arrive at a diversity ranking, an independent council of food industry executives evaluated a wide variety of measures. The council examined ratings by external media, including *Prepared Foods, Working Mothers, Business Week, Good Housekeeping, Black Enterprise, Hispanic, The Advocate, Forbes* and *Fortune.* It also studied both advocacy and research in Ed Mickens's *The 100 Best Companies for Gay Men and Lesbians* (1994), Lawrence Otis Graham's *The Best Companies for Minorities* (1993), and *The 100 Best*

T A B L E   1–3

Correlation Between Diversity Performance and Financial Performance of 10 Food Companies

Time Period	Correlation	Significance Level
1 year	.32	Not significant
5 years	.79	5%
10 years	.84	1%

Source: In-house research at the Pillsbury Company, Robert Hayles, Ph.D., June 1994.

Companies to Work for in America, by Robert Levering and Milton Moskovitz (1994). Within the food industry, council members compared diversity training, numbers of women and people of color, minority and female purchasing programs, and opinions from corporate college recruiters. All these data were used to rank the 10 food companies according to diversity excellence.

The findings clearly indicated that the food companies with the best diversity practices were also the best financial performers. Table 1–3 displays the results of rank-order correlations for one-, five- and 10-year periods.

Market diversity can be defined as work to create new and more market niches, as well as that evolving from efforts to serve existing diverse market segments more effectively.

3M provides an excellent example of a company that deals successfully with diverse markets and cultures. Its Post-It brand notes sell around the world. But consider for a moment how differently this product is configured to meet its myriad markets: In Japan the notes are long and narrow, allowing for vertical writing patterns. In continental Europe the 3″ × 5″ inch format dominates, since this size most easily accommodates European languages that tend to be more expansive than English. The conciseness of English is reflected in the 3″ × 3″ pad most popular in the United States and Great Britain.

The type of global market diversity exemplified by 3M shows in global partnerships and business alliances as well as in simple international expansion. Take for example an American company that is expanding its operations to another country. The U.S. company must allow the other nation's culture and values to influence and guide its overall business practices. It would be arrogant—and foolish—to assume that what works well in the U.S. will work well elsewhere.

When judged by American standards, for instance, one company found the business practices of its overseas workforce to be less than ethical. Realistically, however, certain things simply could not get done overseas by traditional American channels and procedures. After many meetings, much debate, and many false starts, the American executives came to the unsettling conclusion that, under some circumstances, they had to be flexible and adjust their values and modify their ethical standards. Only by doing so could they accomplish certain business objectives.

Further evidence of business flexibility comes from the example of American Express Financial Advisors.[12] By education, understanding, and commitment to partnership, this company acknowledged and supported its gay and lesbian employees.*

When diversity initiatives began at American Express Financial Advisors, gay and lesbian issues were not included. However, as diversity became the company standard, management supported the establishment of a gay and lesbian network. When network members later took part in a gay/lesbian parade—wearing highly visible company T-shirts—a public uproar ensued. People outraged by the company's "endorsing the gay and lesbian lifestyle" were vocal and active about taking their business elsewhere.

Nevertheless, American Express Financial Advisors held firm in supporting its employees. In doing so, it found that it did indeed lose a certain customer segment. On the other hand, its high-visibility stand also attracted new clients. Heterosexuals supportive of gay and lesbian rights, and other gay and lesbian community members were inspired to purchase the company's services.

For American Express Financial Advisors, a commitment to diversity produced a new market niche and focus: the substantial gay and lesbian buying community that had not previously sought out the firm but now considered it a preferred provider of financial services.[13]

---

*The most advanced organizations with respect to diversity initiatives also include bisexual, transsexual, and transgender individuals when addressing gay/lesbian issues. These three additional groups do not consider themselves to be heterosexual or homosexual and often seek recognition along with gays and lesbians.

OBJECTORS AND RESISTORS

In discussions and presentations arguing for diversity a small percentage of participants usually disagrees or objects to the evidence. A typical objection is that the presenter for diversity is a woman or a person of color and therefore has a vested interest that leads to a bending of the truth.

In reality, these disagreeing or objecting participants may be threatened by or emotionally set against diversity. To accept the logic of diversity-positive arguments would push these participants to engage in diversity work themselves. However, a mindset that resists diversity can filter out evidence in its favor, even when the evidence comes from "majority" presenters and appears in respected traditional sources such as *Business Week* and *The Wall Street Journal*. Such resistance is emotional, not intellectual.

Providing references to original sources is an appropriate first method to counter this resistance, but it needs to be done with respect, persistence, support, and patience. Moving beyond facts, the next approach to addressing such responses involves direct emotional appeals: The speaker or facilitator must connect with the deep values that most people hold (e.g., fairness and equity) and link those values with diversity. One can also ask whether the objectors already care for or love people who are different. Finally, diversity's inclusive nature and definition must be emphasized and demonstrated. Avoid arguing, attacking, and criticizing. When you push too hard, resistors will push back.

From the research, data, and anecdotes cited earlier it is clear that respecting and valuing diversity provides tangible and intangible benefits alike for individuals, groups, and organizations. In those few organizations that have moved beyond race and gender and stressed an even more broadly inclusive process, participants now are beginning to understand the breadth of the diversity concept. People in these organizations are moving along the continuum from apathy through uncertainty to active exploration.

Movement beyond existing initiatives requires new definitions and rationales for diversity. Diversity efforts of the future must look, feel, and act very different from those of the past and present. In this context, the remainder of this book describes models, paths, and perspectives for the implementation of diversity processes. It is written to help achieve real and lasting changes with measurable results for individuals, groups, and organizations.

SUMMARY

- Personal diversity work involves head, hand, and heart—what we know, do, and feel.
- Doing diversity work increases personal and professional effectiveness.
- Group or team synergies are made possible by member diversity.
- Organizations that maintain and value diversity are less likely to make business blunders caused by not understanding their markets, customers, or clients.
- Diverse teams tend to outperform homogeneous teams, especially on complex tasks.
- Organizations that conduct effective diversity work are measurably more productive and profitable.
- Individuals who do not accept the research-based business case for diversity are probably emotionally opposed and may respond more favorably to emotional appeals.
- Pull, don't push, to win participants for diversity work.

NOTES

1. Milton Bennett's model on Developing Intercultural Sensitivity describes this growth and is summarized in the section on models for individual development.
2. Taylor Cox, Jr., *Cultural Diversity in Organizations: Theory, Research, and Practice* (San Francisco: Berrett-Koehler, 1993).
3. There are hundreds of these examples. Many are documented by David A. Ricks, *Big Business Blunders: Mistakes in Multinational Marketing,* (Homewood, Ill.: Dow Jones-Irwin, 1983) and *Blunders in International Business* (Blackwell, 1993).
4. Observed by V. Robert Hayles while working in the food industry.
5. Harry Triandis, Eleanor Hall, and Robert Ewen, "Member Heterogeneity and Dyadic Creativity," *Human Relations* 18 (1965): 33–55.

6. Robert C. Ziller, "Homogeneity and Heterogeneity of Group Membership" in *Experimental Psychology*, ed. C. G. McClintock (New York: Holt, Rinehart and Winston, 1972), 385–411.

7. *Business Week*, 21 Aug. 1989.

8. Robert L. Latimer, "The Impact of Diversity on Team Performance," *Connections* 1 (1996).

9. Robert Levering, *A Great Place to Work* (New York: Random House, 1989); Dennis J. Kravetz, *The Human Resources Revolution* (San Francisco: Jossey-Bass, 1989).

10. Heidrick & Struggles, Inc., *The New Diversity: Women and Minorities on Corporate Boards* (Heidrick & Struggles, Inc., 1993).

11. *The Wall Street Journal*, 4 May 1993.

12. This example was provided by Richard S. Gaskins, Vice President, Diversity Resource Center, American Express Financial Advisors.

13. Ibid.

2

CHAPTER

Diversity Defined

This brief chapter sets the stage and provides an overview for initiating diversity work in organizations. It establishes common definitions and covers key related concepts for successfully doing diversity work.

DEFINITIONS OF DIVERSITY

One of the most powerful concepts underlying successful diversity initiatives is a *broad, inclusive definition* of diversity. The Pillsbury Co. simply calls diversity "all the ways in which we differ."[1] Most organizations with reputations for excellence in this area either use a succinct definition like Pillsbury's or a long list of differences that usually concludes with the phrase ". . . and other individual differences" or words to that effect.

Listed below are definitions from several organizations with strong diversity programs:

- **3M:** "Respecting our differences. . . Maximizing our individual potentials and valuing our uniqueness while synergizing our collective talents and experiences for the growth and success of 3M."

- **Honeywell:** "The belief, philosophy and recognition that each individual is unique and valuable, melding into and conflicting with established norms. The necessary skills and energy for business success will be drawn from this array of people. Therefore, diversity is a given that will be with us throughout our professional and social lives."
- **Defense Equal Opportunity Management Institute:** "The otherness, or those human qualities that are different from our own and which make people different along one or several dimensions, such as ethnicity, age, gender, race, etc."
- **Northern States Power Co.:** "Inclusiveness . . . respect for the individual . . . valuing and capitalizing on differences for the benefit of the business, customers, community and employees!"
- **Monsanto Agricultural Group:** "Diversity refers to all the ways in which people differ and the effect of those differences on our thinking and behavior."
- **The St. Paul Companies:** "Managing diversity means fostering an environment where all employees can contribute to their fullest potential to achieve our business objectives."
- **Ford Motor Co.:** "Diversity in the work place includes *all differences* that define each of us as unique individuals. Differences such as culture, ethnicity, race, gender, nationality, age, religion, disability, sexual orientation, education, experiences, opinions and beliefs are just some of the distinctions that we each bring to the work place. By understanding, respecting and valuing these differences, we can capitalize on the benefits that diversity brings to the Company."
- **Medtronic, Inc.:** "To achieve a diverse workforce, Medtronic must recognize, accept and respect individual differences and be aware that these differences affect the way employees work and interact with each other. Each person is influenced by characteristics such as age, gender, nationality, physical ability, race, sexual orientation, culture, values, attitudes and behavioral style which make her or him uniquely different from others."

- **U.S. Department of Energy:** "Diversity at the Department of Energy has internal, external and global meanings. It encompasses all differences in individuals and groups, moving well beyond race and gender to the broadest definition of inclusiveness for employees, contractors, suppliers and our customers. Diversity at the Department of Energy is about establishing superior performance."

When inclusive definitions are coupled with consistent actions, everyone feels that diversity work will benefit them.

While broad inclusiveness reduces resistance and prevents backlash, it often results in complaints regarding issues of gender and race. Diversity leaders are sometimes accused of diluting much-needed work on racism and sexism by discussing "*all* the ways in which we differ." Typical comments during general or introductory education and training sessions are: "This is a waste of time", "When are you going to deal with the real issues?", and "You're letting white males off too easy."

These feelings must be respected; however, when such complaints occur—or before they occur—it must be made clear that broad inclusion will enhance the work on race and gender, not dilute it. Initiating diversity by dealing exclusively with race and gender often causes disengagement on the part of those who most need to face race and gender issues. In short, initiating diversity work with broadly inclusive definitions leads to greater positive change among more individuals. All of us must do this work; all of us will benefit from it.

> In Germany, the Nazis first came for the Communists, and I didn't speak up, because I wasn't a Communist. Then they came for the Jews, and I didn't speak up, because I wasn't a Jew. Then they came for the trade unionists, and I didn't speak up because I wasn't a trade unionist. Then they came for the Catholics, and I didn't speak up because I was a Protestant. Then they came for me, and by that time, there was no one left to speak for me.
>
> *The Rev. Martin Niemoeller*[2]

In the language of psychology, effective personal development addresses knowledge, behavior, and feelings. Personal diversity work is also developmental. Often, however, personal development takes place in an organizational context. There,

FIGURE 2-1

Personal Diversity Work

$$H^3$$

Head (mandatory)	×	Hand (mandatory)	×	Heart (optional)

Source: Robert Hayles, Grand Metropolitan, and Pillsbury, 1993

increasing one's knowledge and addressing one's appropriate or inappropriate behavior may be mandatory.

Addressing feelings and emotions also leads to growth, but this is an aspect of personal development that cannot be commanded in groups or organizations. Fortunately, if one captures any two of the three components—head, hand, and heart—positive overall change is likely to result. The best diversity interventions encompassing individuals and groups include all three aspects, with "heart" work being encouraged, supported, rewarded, and assisted, but not required.

SIMILARITIES AND DIFFERENCES: A DUAL FOCUS

Though the labels used to describe this work (diversity, differences, pluralism, etc.) suggest that we focus only on ways that people differ, it is critical to explore similarities too. Finding and sharing commonalities helps build relationships and sets the stage for viewing differences constructively. All human beings share some commonalities. These similarities help us get along and use our differences in creative synergy.

The question of universal human qualities has been studied for centuries. The most enduring work indicates that the ways people vary from each other are highly consistent. Examples include common factors in human intelligence and cognitive processes, common dimensions on which cultures vary, and personality styles rooted in Jungian psychology—the well-known Myers-Briggs traits, for example.

Survival is one measure of human intelligence. While all people strive to survive, they do so in different ways and therefore demonstrate the "same" intelligence with different behaviors. All humans take in and process information. We vary in our preferences for sensory modality (sight, sound, touch, taste, smell), level of detail, sequence, phasing or spacing, and mediums for receiving and transmitting. All humans express the same emotions, but often do so differently. At least one international business executive—Lucio Rizzi, president of Pillsbury International (a division of The Pillsbury Company)—believes that culture is simply an overlay of differences on a common human core.[3]

A recent scholarly essay by Rushworth M. Kidder lists "common values" as love, truthfulness, fairness, freedom, unity, tolerance, responsibility, and respect for life.[4] Reflecting on this list, we see great variation in how these values are expressed around the globe. We are different and the same.

UNITY WITHOUT UNIFORMITY

Frequently during diversity work individuals ask, "Why can't we all just be the same or at least treat everyone the same? Why can't we have one set of rules for everyone? Why can't we just talk about similarities? Aren't we all in this together?"

The answer to the last question is yes. The answer to the other questions depends on whether you want average-to-declining levels of group and organizational performance or high performance and growth instead. As delineated in Chapter 1, uniformity brings mediocre performance, marketplace blunders, and less innovation. On the other hand, diversity, along with common goals, brings synergy.

It has somewhere been well said that unity plus diversity 1 + I + uno = 4 or more.

SAMENESS, FAIRNESS, AND EFFECTIVENESS

As noted above, creativity and innovation are difficult to achieve without diversity. If we accept this idea, we must also accept that it is neither fair nor effective to treat everyone the same. Consider an example of twins with different interests. Pretend that your son Ariel loves music, math, and movies. His twin brother William loves art, architecture, and archeology. In this situation, it is unlikely that you would give both sons the same gifts, education, or feedback. Rather, you would attempt to give different gifts of similar value, different forms of education designed to develop the unique talents of each child, and feedback consistent with each boy's individual goals. Treating them identically would be a disservice to both.

Further examples from human situations are useful to consider: Offering academic courses only during the day denies access to students who must work those hours. Fixed working hours make employment difficult for families with varying dependent care needs. Teaching only through written materials denies education to those who learn better by listening than by reading. Requiring everyone to eat the same foods impairs the health of those with differing dietary needs.

Having said that, however, there are times when identical treatment *is* appropriate: Employees doing the same work with comparable competence, should be equally paid. Individuals buying the same service or product under similar conditions and terms should pay the same price. Loan applicants who have similar assets and credit records should be charged the same interest rate. Criminals who commit the same crime under similar conditions should receive the same sentences.

In these cases, if the treatment accorded these individuals is not even-handed, complaints are legitimate. And, in the real world, people in similar situations are sometimes treated differently on the basis of gender, race, age, or other characteristics. That is discrimination—unfair, wrong, and in many parts of the world illegal.

EMERGING DIMENSIONS OF DIVERSITY

Organizations that effectively advance their diversity initiatives have two common characteristics:

1. They emphasize a broad definition of diversity: *all* the ways in which we differ.
2. They seamlessly integrate diversity management principles into *all* aspects of the organization, including:
   - The design of structures that support diversity (structural diversity).
   - The design of systems that support diversity (systemic diversity).

- Marketing efforts that consistently focus on creating, understanding, and serving diverse market segments.
- Thoughtful management of the dynamics of global diversity: methods of doing business in other countries; factors influencing employment in other countries; and preparation of employees who will work in other countries.

Thorough integration is the key. None of these dimensions stands alone. Each consideration supports another, and overall effectiveness is determined by the extent to which the diversity initiative addresses each dimension. Following are specific definitions and discussion of these new diversity dimensions.

Structural Diversity

Structure refers to the overall organization and function of a company's business units. Among factors influencing structural diversity are sales and marketing operations, work teams, a philosophy of centralization or decentralization, and the presence or absence of diversity networks.

Diversity work to maximize structural diversity:

- Creates structures that allow for synergy between people, processes, and results.
- Emphasizes flexibility in systems and procedures that take into account the needs of various groups and of the diverse workforce as a whole.
- Supports systems and procedures that encourage creativity and innovation.

The Shamrock organization[5] illustrates this type of flexibility. Within the company are support structures for groups of employees who are managed differently, paid differently, and organized differently.

Market Diversity

As we defined it in Chapter 1, market diversity refers to the creation and support of new and more disparate market niches, and the alignment of products or services to the needs of the end user.

Diversity work supports market diversity by:

- Broadening the organization's perspective, allowing it to more quickly recognize new market opportunities.
- Sensitizing people in the organization to issues of culture, values, and beliefs as they establish and support new markets.

Global Diversity

Global diversity refers to the ability to handle challenges that arise when employees from different countries work together. Examples include immigrants working for a U.S. company and American employees working abroad for a foreign subsidiary.

Diversity work to manage these global dynamics:

- Encourages intercultural cooperation among employees.
- Creates an environment that supports diverse perspectives.
- Designs structures and systems that take into account the values and beliefs underlying various business practices.
- Designs structures, systems, and organizational initiatives that consider and respond to diverse perspectives.

Here is an example of global diversity: An American manufacturing company felt confused when its Hmong workers did not respond as readily as more Westernized employees to the company's new empowerment initiative. On examination it was found that the Hmong had no concept of worker empowerment. Culturally, this group was uncomfortable with the idea of individual empowerment. Most preferred that their supervisors give them direction and tell them what to do.

As organizations discover the many benefits of diversity management, they will get the most from their efforts by consistent focus and integration.

SUMMARY

- State-of-the-art definitions of diversity basically see it as "all the ways in which we differ."

- Diversity management refers to the many ways that diversity work can be used to assist an organization to achieve its business goals and objectives.
- The best organizational definitions refer to individual uniqueness, inclusivity, and *all* differences.
- Diversity work involves what we know (mandatory change), how we behave (also mandatory), and how we feel (optional but very powerful work).
- The emotional dimension of diversity training should be undertaken on a voluntary and professionally facilitated basis.
- Diversity work must address both similarities *and* differences.
- Unity without uniformity.
- Sameness in treatment is not always either fair or effective, yet there are times when identical treatment *is* appropriate.
- Two emerging dimensions of diversity are: (1) a broad definition of diversity and (2) seamless integration of diversity management principles into *all* aspects of the organization.

NOTES

1. Phrase used in Pillsbury's diversity material.
2. Quotation by Reverend Martin Niemoller seen in many public places.
3. Personal communication to Robert Hayles.
4. Rushworth M. Kidder, "Universal Human Values: Finding an Ethical Common Ground" The Futurist 28, no.4 (1994): 8–13.
5. Described by Charles Handy, *The Age of Unreason* (Boston: Harvard Business School Press, 1990), 87–115.

3

Models of Individual and Group Development

The current knowledge base for diversity work includes many models to guide efforts at the individual, group, and organizational levels. A few of these models are well-developed and sufficient to provide more than nominal guidance. The models are powerful in part because they present specific states or stages through which individuals, groups, and organizations move as they grow and become more effective.

These models have been used for assessment and diagnosis, as well as to guide the design of interventions in The Pillsbury Company, Ford Motor Company, Mobil Oil, Allstate, and Amoco. The concept of developmental stages, fundamental to the study of human growth, is inherent in these models. It embodies three basic principles.

First, human beings all develop by moving through predictable stages that can be reliably described. Second, if the work required at a given stage is not completed, further development will be hindered and regression to an earlier stage is likely. Third, the stage of behavior visible to the outside world varies across issues, but the progression of development regarding each issue remains predictable. It is this consistency and predictability that allows diversity professionals to design work and tasks that efficiently stimulate advancement from one stage to the next.

This chapter cites and highlights a few of the excellent and available individual and group development models. Examples have been included to show how state-of-the-art diversity work can be guided by a particular model. Following the descriptions of the models, specific recommended actions are noted. Organizational development models will be discussed in Chapter 4.

INDIVIDUAL DEVELOPMENT MODELS

Bennett Model: Developing Intercultural Sensitivity

Milton J. Bennett's widely recognized model for individual development is shown in Figure 3–1.[1] Even though the label for this model says "intercultural" sensitivity, the basic concepts are applicable to many other ways in which people differ. Its application to a wide range of differences is described below.

Ethnocentric States

Stage 1: Denial of Difference

"London is just like Paris: lots of people and noise."

In the ethnocentric state, there is no recognition of cultural or other differences. Primarily because of isolation or intentional separation, the individual does not have sufficient categories to notice differences. He or she attributes intelligence or personality to deficiency or culturally deviant behavior. There is a tendency to show extreme prejudice and to dehumanize people seen as outsiders.

FIGURE 3–1

Developing Intercultural Sensitivity: A Model

Denial	Defense	Minimization	Acceptance	Adaptation	Integration
Ethnocentric Stages			*Ethnorelative Stages*		

Source: Milton J. Bennett. "Towards a Developmental Model of Intercultural Sensitivity" in Michael Paige (editor), *Education for the Intercultural Experience.* Yarmouth, Maine: Intercultural Press, 1993.

Interventions:
- Should be designed primarily to help people at this level recognize differences without making negative interpretations.
- Diversity in food, travel, arts, music, and entertainment is suggested.
- Explicit behavior guidelines are also useful.

Stage 2: Defense Against Difference

"Immigrants make good workers; they don't communicate well enough to be managers."

People at this level recognize differences and evaluate them negatively. The greater the differences, the more negative the evaluation. People at this level often behave as if threatened. Differences are denigrated, and negative stereotyping occurs.

Reversal also occurs at this level. This is a tendency to see another culture as superior while negatively evaluating one's own.

Interventions:
- Focus on similarities.
- Show the good things shared by different cultures, groups, and individuals.
- Emphasize commonalities without arguing about whether different means good, bad, or just not the same.
- Doing work with the Myers–Briggs Type Indicator might be useful.
- Explicit behavior guidelines continue to be useful.

Stage 3: Minimization of Difference

"Jane, you're very good at strategy. You think like a man."

People at this level recognize and accept superficial differences, such as physical appearance or eating customs, while holding that all human beings are essentially the same. The emphasis at this level is on the similarity of people and the commonality of basic values (i.e., "Everyone is essentially like us."). The person at this stage is unable to accept someone as being different and simultaneously "equal" or at least as good as oneself. In the example, the speaker was genuinely trying to say something positive about Jane. He or she was just unable to see Jane as different (i.e., female) *and* good at strategic thinking.

Interventions:

- Moving beyond this stage involves a significant conceptual shift from clear (either/or) principles to a perspective that is not so absolute (relativism).
- Guided explorations of individual life experiences with people who are different and successful can provide significant insights.
- Simulations can be fun and educational.
- Hearing personal stories and building relationships with people who are different facilitates movement.
- Role playing the part of someone different is also worthwhile.

Ethnorelative States

Stage 4: Acceptance of Difference

"I accept that people who prefer intuition are different from those who prefer analysis. We'll just have to learn to work together."

This level is characterized by recognition and appreciation of differences in behavior and values. These differences are accepted as viable alternative ways to organize human existence and function successfully in the world.

Interventions:

- Emphasize recognition and respect for differences.
- Practice using different communication styles.
- Learn a new language.
- Focus on acceptance while beginning to build respect.
- Active engagement and participation are important for learning at this stage.

Stage 5: Adaptation to Difference

"In order to communicate successfully with my child, I need to think from her perspective and incorporate the appropriate emotional messages."

At this level individuals are developing communication skills that enable effective communication among people who are different (all of us). Adaptations include the effective use of empathy and shifting one's frame of reference in order to understand and be understood.

Interventions:

- Individuals at this level require increasingly challenging opportunities to practice and use their developing competencies in working with people who are different.
- Development of empathy is encouraged.
- Spending time in "the other person's wheelchair" can be beneficial at this point without generating negative evaluations or stereotyping.

Stage 6: Integration of Difference

"I'm at my best when I'm mediating, building bridges between people or groups, and doing mutual interpretation. I sometimes feel like I don't belong in any particular group."

This level is characterized by the internalization of bicultural or multicultural frames of reference. Individuals at this level maintain a definition of identity that is marginal to any particular culture or group.

Interventions:

- Individuals may need help in establishing a self "core" or "kernel."
- Assist the individual in locating and networking with others who feel this way.
- Encourage the individual to spend time developing clarity regarding his or her own personal values.

While the Bennett model was designed for thinking about intercultural issues, it is generally applicable to the design of broader diversity initiatives. It is useful in helping individuals develop their human interaction abilities. We have, therefore, used examples that go beyond cultural differences. *Because everyone is "different" in some ways, every human interaction involves diversity.*

Mendez-Russell Model

Another model for examining individual development was created by Armida Mendez-Russell. This model is explicitly applicable to a broad range of differences, beyond the cultural. It is based on a philosophy of personal diversity work that requires attention to the head, hand, and heart. It addresses knowledge, behavior, and feelings using four categories of exploration. Within each of these categories there are two topics for deeper exploration. The structure of this model is shown in the following table.

Categories Explored	Deeper Exploration
Knowledge (Head)	Stereotype
	Factual information
Understanding (Heart)	Awareness
	Empathy
Acceptance (Hand and Heart)	Tolerance
	Respect
Behavior (Hand and Heart)	Self-awareness
	Interpersonal skills

As one moves through and grows in each of the four categories, a higher developmental level is achieved.

Additional Models

Another line of individual development models comes from work on identity. The "Black Identity Transformation Model" (W. E. Cross, 1971) has five stages:[2]

1. Pre-encounter
2. Encounter
3. Immersion-emersion
4. Internalization
5. Internalization-commitment

A model proposed by Angela Airall (1992) is called "Racial Identity Development for Whites." She also identifies five stages of development:[3]

1. Naiveté
2. Acceptance

3. Resistance

4. Redefinition

5. Internalization

Steve Hanamura (Hanamura Consulting) distinguishes eight stages of individual development regarding diversity:[4]

1. Discovery

2. Anger

3. Withdrawal and self-doubt

4. Seclusion

5. Rebirth

6. The need to belong

7. The con artist

8. Self-actualization

Finally, Terry L. Cross (1988) describes development in six stages:[5]

1. Destructiveness

2. Incapacity

3. Blindness

4. Pre-Competence

5. Basic Competence

6. Proficiency

Individual diagnosis must be done to determine the stage of development prior to recommending action. Additional instruments for diagnosing developmental stages are currently in development or being used experimentally. More research-based tools for diagnosis are likely to be available within a few years.

SUGGESTIONS FOR INDIVIDUAL DEVELOPMENT

An organization cannot make respect for, and leverage of, diversity a reality without the active participation of each of its members. Individuals within the organization must accept personal responsibility, be held accountable, and embark on personal journeys of their own. Likewise, they must work in partnership with the organization to achieve its goals, simultaneously engaging in both personal and organizational diversity work. We offer here some suggestions drawn from long experience:

Start with Yourself

The first step is to examine and assess where you are with respect to diversity. A thorough assessment examines personal opinions about diversity as well as ways in which attitudes about diversity influence your interactions within the organization.

In this first step, examine your current knowledge and understanding of those who are different from you. Ask yourself such questions as:

- What do I know about a particular individual or group?
- What assumptions do I hold or make about this person or members of this group?
- How do I feel about this person or these individuals?

Next examine your ability to accept, respect, and value others who are different from you. Ask yourself:

- How tolerant am I?
- Do I demonstrate respect for others or am I sometimes disrespectful of them and their points of view?
- Do I feel and show authentic positive regard for others?

Once you have considered these questions, develop greater awareness of your own behaviors. Learn to recognize your reactions to those who are different from you. When meeting others for the first time, ask yourself: Do I behave or react in a manner that may be inappropriate or offensive?

Now examine the ways in which you work with those who are different. Ask yourself: Do I possess the skills needed to work effectively with others who have different values, beliefs, styles, behaviors, or thought patterns?

Chart a Course for Self-Development

After a thorough self-assessment, the next step is to make a specific plan of action—as well as a commitment to follow the plan.

Begin by listing and building on your personal strengths in working with and relating to others. Are you naturally a good listener? Do you possess a special ability to develop trust or to understand and paraphrase the thoughts and feelings of others?

As part of your plan, identify some specific things you will do to expand your knowledge and understanding of others. Start with activities that are challenging but not outside your personal comfort zone. While you might not feel comfortable inviting members of a particular group to your home for dinner, you might be willing to attend a cultural event that is outside your everyday experience.

The second step in your plan might involve expanding your circle of colleagues and friends. To do this you will have to actively search out opportunities to meet and get to know new people.

Keep each risk manageable. When engaging in new activities, you are likely to experience some discomfort or sense of uneasiness. If you feel a great deal of anxiety, you may have chosen an activity that exceeds your present level of readiness for new experiences.

Assist Your Organization's Diversity Process

Call attention to factors that hinder progress or are inconsistent with stated goals and objectives. Speak out when you observe inappropriate behavior. Challenge organizational systems, practices, and procedures that exclude or marginalize individuals or members of specific groups.

GROUP DEVELOPMENT MODELS

There are two basic strategies for group level work. One is to simply examine the distribution of individuals in the organization and develop initiatives that will capture most of those in the group with which you are working. Since diagnostic tools supporting this strategy are somewhat limited, this approach draws heavily on experience and judgment.

Another approach is to complete a thorough needs analysis, identifying specific issues and determining goals with respect to each group. Once the issues and needs are clear, you can address them while applying what is known about ideal learning environments.

If the goal is reduction of prejudice, there is a small and cogent body of literature to guide the work. The best known model is often called the Contact Hypothesis, clearly described by Yehuda Amir two decades ago.[6] The strategy here aims to reduce prejudice by creating ideal contacts among individuals within the group. Most of these conditions can be created in education and training settings. Many can also be created in work and social environments.

According to Amir, ideal contact conditions for reducing prejudice include:

- Equal status within the group.
- The group has or is experiencing a positive perception of another group.
- Other majority group members are involved.
- The group is or will be engaging in an activity requiring intergroup cooperation.
- The situation entails interdependence or superordinate goals.
- Contact is more intimate than casual.
- Authority and/or the social climate promote intergroup contact.
- Contact is pleasant and rewarding.

While Amir's hypothesis was developed within the context of work on race and ethnicity, it is clearly applicable to other differences.

SUGGESTIONS FOR GROUP DEVELOPMENT

Groups, teams, and work units play a vital role in furthering an organization's diversity initiative. By presenting positive models, testing new ideas, and formalizing strategies that include rather than exclude, they move the organization forward in a way that is often impossible for individuals working independently.

Teams and work groups can support and enhance diversity by recognizing and constructively addressing issues of difference within their working environment. Diverse work groups should take special care to develop mechanisms for spotlighting divisive issues such as communication breakdowns, hidden agendas, and unstated assumptions.

Ideally, diverse teams and work groups should cooperatively establish behavioral norms, operating procedures, and ways to resolve conflict before addressing their stated task or business objective. Establishing operating norms and addressing the team's diversity *before* addressing the task ensures that the group will be able to maintain its primary focus. Groups that focus too quickly on goal accomplishment often fail to develop a team identity. When this identity is missing, the group may lose its focus and fail to accomplish its primary task.

Diverse groups also have a responsibility to educate others by sharing their challenges and successes. This can be done by identifying factors that are likely to hinder any group's progress and by sharing strategies, processes, and practices that have been proven to contribute to group success. Representatives from successful groups can share their knowledge by serving as guest facilitators or consultants to newly formed teams or groups that are experiencing diversity-related difficulties. Representatives from successful teams often find it easier to identify ineffective systems or inappropriate leadership practices.

All groups within the organization should strive to create models and systems that focus on inclusion, trust, and mutual respect. Systems and practices that prove to be successful should be mapped, formalized, and shared throughout the organization.

SUMMARY

- Individuals and groups go through predictable stages in their development.
- Failure to complete the work at a particular stage of development inhibits sustained growth.
- Models of individual and group development can be used to diagnose and assess performance.
- Developmental models guide the design and implementation of actions to improve performance.
- Suggestions for individual personal work include assessing oneself, reviewing behavioral guidelines, role playing

someone different from you, getting feedback from others, and engaging in open dialogue with trusted friends or colleagues.

- The group conditions under which prejudice is most likely to be reduced are equal status, positive perceptions, majority-group involvement, cooperative activities, interdependence, intimate contact, support of authorities, pleasant or rewarding contact.
- Team-building activities enhance the positive impacts of diversity on team performance.

NOTES

1. Source: Milton J. Bennett. "Towards a Developmental Model of Intercultural Sensitivity" in Michael Paige (editor), Education for the Intercultural Experience. Yarmouth, Maine: Intercultural Press, 1993.

2. W. E. Cross, "The Negro-to-Black Conversion Experience: Towards a Psychology of Black Liberation," Black World, 1971, vol. 20, pp. 13–27.

3. Angela M. Airall, "How Whites Can Grow in Racial Identity," Cultural Diversity at Work (newsletter), Seattle, WA, September 1992, vol. 5, no. 1.

4. Steve Hanamura, "Developmental Stages of Diversity: Celebrating Oneness," Hanamura Consulting, Portland, Oregon, 1996.

5. Terry L. Cross, "Services to Minority Populations: Cultural Competence Continuum," Focal Point: The Bulletin of the Research and Training Center, Portland Minority Project, vol. 3, no. 1, Fall, 1988.

6. Yehuda, Amir, "The Role of Intergroup Contact in Change of Prejudice and Ethnic Relations" chapter 8, pp. 245-308, in Phyllis A. Katz (editor), Towards the Elimination of Racism. New York: Pergamon Press Inc., 1976.

4
CHAPTER

Organizational Development Models

Many models have been developed and are available to guide diversity work at the organizational level. Some noted developers include: Bailey Jackson, Rita Hardiman, and Mark Chesler; Monica Armour; Judith Katz and Frederick A. Miller; and Ellen O'Neill working with Nancy Okerlund. Their models are all developmental and include clearly identifiable stages, many of which parallel the individual models described earlier. Like the individual- and group-level models we discussed in Chapter 3, these organizational-level models have been used to assess, diagnose, and prescribe appropriate actions to move an organization to the next (higher) stage of development. Organizations using these organizational-level models to guide their diversity initiatives include Amoco, Pillsbury, Mobil Oil, Ford, Oakland Community College, Burger King, and J.C. Penney.

Diversity professionals can maximize their positive impact and effectiveness by simultaneously applying models at the individual, group, and organizational levels. As individuals progress through stages of development under conditions created to reduce human bias, the capacity of the organization to function in unity without uniformity continues to grow. Human behavior then complements organizational changes (systems, structures, policies, etc.), producing lasting positive outcomes.

As we examine organizational-level models, it also becomes evident that individual and group behaviors are indicators or reflections of the stage of development at which the organization is functioning. Therefore the models presented below can be used along with individual and group models to diagnose and prescribe appropriate actions.

Three organizational models are presented below. They are followed by a synthesizing summary. The summary describes early, middle, and advanced developmental stages in terms of characteristics of each stage and actions that are effective in moving the organization forward. Resources for these recommended actions include work associated with the models, the benchmarking and best-practices research of Ann Morrison (1992)[1], and the authors' experiences applying such tools.

ORGANIZATIONAL DEVELOPMENT MODELS

The first model was developed by Nancy Adler (1980).[2] As shown in Figure 4–1, this model powerfully conveys the concept of moving from a situation in which one organizational culture is dominant to one where pluralism and synergy are more evident.

Adler's thinking about the special features of organizations that value diversity (multicultural or pluralistic) stimulated development of more detailed models, along with studies of how such organizations can be created. For example, Jackson, Hardiman, and Chesler (1981)[3] described monocultural, nondiscriminating, and multicultural levels of development. Most of the models in use today build on their seminal work.

Working extensively throughout the United States and building on the work of Jackson and his colleagues, Katz and Miller then developed the model depicted in Figure 4–2.

During the 1980s other models expanded both the range of applicability available to practitioners and the choice of vocabulary and style. The next model shown in Figure 4–3, was developed by Monica Armour. It emerged from work in several regions of the world and blends the conceptual thinking from Adler with the stage model of Jackson and his colleagues.[4]

FIGURE 4-1

Creating Cultural Synergy

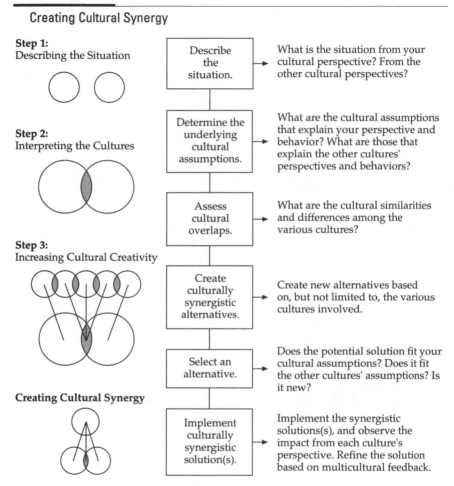

Step 1:
Describing the Situation

| Describe the situation. | What is the situation from your cultural perspective? From the other cultural perspectives? |

Step 2:
Interpreting the Cultures

| Determine the underlying cultural assumptions. | What are the cultural assumptions that explain your perspective and behavior? What are those that explain the other cultures' perspectives and behaviors? |

| Assess cultural overlaps. | What are the cultural similarities and differences among the various cultures? |

Step 3:
Increasing Cultural Creativity

| Create culturally synergistic alternatives. | Create new alternatives based on, but not limited to, the various cultures involved. |

| Select an alternative. | Does the potential solution fit your cultural assumptions? Does it fit the other cultures' assumptions? Is it new? |

Creating Cultural Synergy

| Implement culturally synergistic solution(s). | Implement the synergistic solutions(s), and observe the impact from each culture's perspective. Refine the solution based on multicultural feedback. |

In general, each model covers early, middle, and late stages of development. Although each has its own distinctive vocabulary, the conceptual meanings are similar. In the following sections each stage is discussed separately, with suggested implementation ideas for leading organizations forward. Practitioners must select specific interventions that fit the unique situation and culture of the organization undertaking the change.

FIGURE 4–2

The Path: From a Monocultural Club to an Inclusive Organization

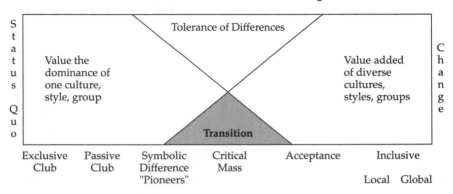

FIGURE 4–3

A Model for Stages of Pluralistic Organization Development

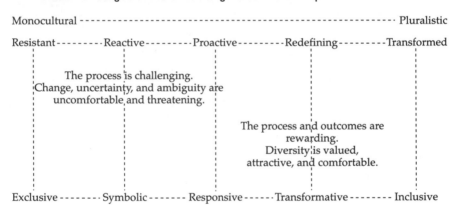

EARLY STAGES

Words like *resistant, exclusive, passive,* and *club* describe organiza-tions in the early stages of development. There are no diversity programs. Segregation is evident. It is likely that visible diversity does not exist. Indeed, invisible diversity remains hidden and no substantial efforts are under way to change the organization's climate or culture. Those who are different from the majority of employees are implicitly or sometimes explicitly discouraged from joining the organization. Diversity is viewed as separate from business planning.

Job advertisements noting that "foreigners need not apply" or observations that "no person over the age of 40 has ever been hired in sales" characterize organizations in these early stages. Today, these organizations stand out for extreme intolerance of diversity issues. Outright hostility is often evident.

Motivation to Act

Motivation to take action during this stage typically comes from four types of pressures:

- Members of the organization (e.g., students, staff, players, associates) express their dissatisfaction through surveys, letters to management, anonymous calls, or information leaks to the press.
- External groups or organizations write, call, complain in the media, or even threaten a boycott.
- Internal members or external bodies (e.g., government, unsuccessful applicants, civic groups) formally litigate or file complaints.
- The performance of the organization falls below that of competitors.

Appropriate Interventions

Needs Assessment
There is strong agreement among diversity professionals that a needs assessment or issues identification process must occur early in a diversity initiative. Surveys, focus groups, human resource data analyses, and personnel audits are appropriate first steps. Since this work is difficult without support from senior leaders, efforts to persuade management must precede or accompany the needs assessment.

Team Building
Before an organization's leaders can move forward with diversity, they must learn to work together as a team. Team building often must precede explicit work on diversity.

Leadership Briefing

This briefing covers the basics regarding the what, why, and how of diversity. It is most effective if results from the needs assessment can be included. If the needs assessment has not yet occurred, this briefing can help make the case for doing it. Key messages in the leadership briefing include a broad and inclusive definition of diversity, multiple and compelling rationales for doing diversity work, and fundamentals for doing the work. Fundamentals should cover personal and organizational work, addressing similarities as well as differences, and a focus on unity without uniformity.

An organization's commitment to diversity work frequently begins with the leadership briefing.

Identification of Resources

Time, money, and people must be available to move forward with diversity. At this stage only limited time commitments are likely— a few hours per manager and supervisor or a luncheon presentation for all employees, for example. Money, too, will be limited by the perception of whether diversity can enhance financial and other types of performance.

Unless the organization has diversity professionals already on staff, external people will be needed to help launch the diversity initiative. External expertise is usually necessary to get the work started competently. Internal talent can be developed as the work proceeds; this is critical for long-term cost effectiveness and institutionalizing the work.

Compliance

Traditional compliance work must be continued (or initiated) during this stage. Equal Opportunities and similar programs, which are less proactive than affirmative action or positive discrimination, are appropriate here.

Workshop for All Participants

An introductory session (two to eight hours) for all participants in the organization is effective near the end of the early stage. The workshop contains the same key messages that were covered in the leadership briefing, but is usually designed to be more participative than briefings. Involving everyone in this session helps strengthen the foundation for moving the organization to the next phase.

Human Resource Systems Review
As participants begin their diversity education, the organization will benefit from reviewing all of its people processes. The goal is to remove any barriers to participation for people who are under-represented or invisible in the organization. Proactively creating a healthier climate comes at a later stage. The more modest goal here is merely to remove negative policies and eliminate discriminatory practices.

Be Opportunistic
In every institution there is variation in individual and group motivation for diversity work. Diversity professionals must take full advantage of the desire of a particular senior manager or management group to move faster than others. Pilot and demonstration projects can help light the way for other individuals and organizational units. However, it is not advisable to encourage groups and individuals to move ahead too fast where there is not at least a neutral climate of support.

Vision, Policy, and Plans
After leaders know what diversity is, why it is important, and how it is done, it is time for visions, policies, and plans. These are frequently poor if developed too soon. They must be generated from within with full participation. Taking them "off-the-shelf" or paying an expert to develop them for you is rarely effective.

Further, to reduce resistance and prevent backlash, the key messages (definition, similarities and differences, unity with diversity) must be communicated frequently through multiple channels. Internal resource development must be enhanced as well. This includes focused diversity expertise and awareness and knowledge in the general population that is needed in order to move ahead.

Resolution
If litigation or formally raised complaints occurred in this stage, the issues must be resolved before the organization can move to middle stages. Credibility is critical to sustained involvement. For

issues that are ongoing or potentially problematic, flexible listening processes must be in place, along with opportunities for dialogue. These elements are particularly important with disenfranchised individuals or groups. Sometimes financial rewards or incentives for diversity work and results can be designed at the end of this phase.

MIDDLE STAGES

The middle stages of diversity-related organizational development are described by words like *transition, affirmative action, proactive,* and *responsive.* These stages are also characterized by the increased involvement of larger numbers of people. For instance, both human resources and line management are likely to be involved. Existing networks and employee resource groups are growing and new ones are being formed. Constituents (women, ethnic and culture groups, people with disabilities) may perceive growing competition for critical resources. Reluctance to address issues of sexual orientation, however, is still likely at this stage.

Most organizations in the United States and Canada are in these middle stages. Some organizations in other parts of the world have reached this stage, as well. Examples may be found in Indonesia, Singapore, Malaysia, the Nordic European countries, and parts of South Africa.

Motivation to Act

As organizations enter the middle phases of development, compliance continues to be a significant motivator. Internal complaints typically increase as participants see a chance for positive responses. However, external litigation often declines as individuals and groups no longer find it necessary to go outside the organization to be heard. Internal demand for diversity activities (e.g., support for network groups, visibility advertising, and participation in external events) grows rapidly during these stages.

General demand from the grass roots increases as the number and commitment of volunteers to do diversity work grows. These volunteers, along with others, demand that senior leaders "walk the talk" and honor their words with appropriate deeds. A desire for more than token or symbolic representation of visible differences is often expressed.

During this time, organizations are also likely to be pulled or pushed from the outside. Missed opportunities in the marketplace may become visible now. Often employee resource groups (networks or affinity groups) or competitors draw attention to these missed opportunities.

Bad press often occurs during this time of heightened sensitivity, which in turn creates a need to start proactive media planning. Additional external pressure arises when local organizations or businesses in the same industry launch their own diversity efforts. It's embarrassing to be different in this respect.

Once organizations move into these middle phases, other motivations emerge to propel them forward. These include the results of internal data collection in opinion surveys, focus groups, open-door practices, and other forms of internal communication. These perceptual data are often accompanied by unsatisfactory results in employee retention.

As high visibility turnover occurs among some of the "firsts" (e.g., first social scientist to run a technical organization, first Native American engineer, first Asian supervisor, first male secretary, first woman finance officer), people find energy to deal with retention in proactive ways. Senior leaders begin to feel multiple motivations ranging from diversity being the "right thing to do" to it being "a business issue."

Appropriate Interventions

In the middle stages of development the list of potential actions is substantial. Many are aimed at systems as well as at expansion of the personal diversity work typically conducted in small groups. We discuss several of these potential actions below.

Internal Diversity Leaders

An internal person is often appointed to lead the diversity effort. Frequently, the criteria for selecting this person have been knowledge of the organization, functional expertise (law or human resources), and being a woman or a person of color. However, while gender and race affect one's life experience and perspective, they are not synonymous with competence. Furthermore, diversity competence is not always included in the new job description for diversity leaders. However, when the leader has the appropriate skills or support to obtain them, the appointment serves the organization well.

Feedback and Communication
Systems are set up for ongoing and periodic feedback (perceptual and factual) about the organization's progress regarding diversity. Proactive communication increases to share visions, plans, initiatives, and accomplishments. During the middle stages these assessment and communication activities become integral parts of other organizational work rather than separate sets of tasks.

Personal Work
Personal work is professionally guided exploration of one's own knowledge, behavior, and most important feelings, attitudes, or emotions about specific diversity issues. Personal work is usually done first by senior leaders, then managers, supervisors, and individual contributors.

Once an inclusive definition of diversity is in place, personal work must be done on specific issues identified as significant. This work helps participants translate understanding into more effective behavior. The words and deeds of leaders proactively create the desired inclusive, high-performing environment.

It is usually during this phase that action such as termination for sexual harassment first occurs. Typically, issues of style, gender, color, culture, disability, sexual orientation, departmental or disciplinary function, age, marital status, and religion are on the personal work list. The list is limited only by the creative diversity that exists in humans and their organizations.

Since progress is slow or absent without support from senior leaders, personal diversity work is often the missing link for organizations that seem to get stuck in the middle stages. *Personal work is required in order to move to advanced stages of development.*

Rebalancing Recruitment and Retention
In the middle stages organizations perfect their recruiting skills. They may even conduct searches for students or employees with

an explicit emphasis on diversity, or they may require every slate of candidates to be diverse. As they move through these stages, organizations shift their emphasis from recruitment to retention and upward mobility. Mentoring, tracking, pay equity analyses, exit interviews, and other efforts focused on understanding and managing retention increase at this time. Mentoring also may move from being formal and structured toward being an integral and informal part of the organization's culture.

Look Outside for Recognition
Benchmarking, studying best practices, and competing as a "best" organization are marks of the middle stages. Competition for recognition is often unsuccessful except for the feedback and learning that occurs. Benchmarking and examination of best practices fuel new emphasis on specific programs and broadening of the diversity agenda—usually adding work and family, and perhaps sexual orientation. The organization now knows how far it needs to go to be the best. It also learns during these phases that the standard of excellence is raised each year.

Human Resource System Integration
During the middle stages diversity moves from being a separate element toward being an integral part of all human resource systems. This shift is developmentally appropriate. Diversity cannot be integrated until it has its own foundation that is known to all participants. Nor can a weak diversity foundation be successfully integrated. Integration means that diversity is reflected in all human resource processes from pre-recruitment through post-retirement. It means, for example, that performance regarding diversity becomes a part of the performance appraisal system. Diversity actions and results are often linked with compensation and/or incentives and rewards.

Initiative Linkages
To leverage the impact of diversity work, organizations link their diversity initiatives with other efforts designed to improve performance and quality of life. Examples include quality, change management, reengineering, and cross-functional team building.

Becoming Part of the Organization's Core

During these middle stages organizations begin to make diversity an integral part of their functioning. If the business is education, for example, then faculty, curriculum, and students all use diversity to enhance knowledge and educational experiences. If it is public service, diversity is sought in order to enhance service delivery and promote a positive image in all communities. If it is industry (providing goods and services), then diversity is seen in every business activity from new product development through customer service and even waste disposal. The importance of diversity is at least acknowledged in both the external market and in internal human resource assets.

An Ongoing Compelling Case

Making the case for diversity continues to be required throughout the middle stages. Internal data become more compelling than external information. Quantitative data become more available and are perceived as more influential.

Ongoing Work

Much of the work initiated during earlier stages continues here. Policies need updating and appropriate developmental advancement. For example, the sexual harassment policy becomes a "no harassment" policy that goes beyond gender and has a more inclusive style. Moreover, remaining in compliance with current legislation requires changes such as those needed to meet access requirements for people with disabilities. The pool of internal resources doing diversity work needs continuous development and renewal.

ADVANCED STAGES

The adjectives for the advanced stages include *redefining, transformative, multicultural, pluralistic,* and *inclusive.* Very few organizations have reached this level, and those that have reached this level have typically been engaged in diversity work for a minimum of five to 10 years. Most have been deliberately addressing pluralism for 15 or more years. We do not mean to suggest, however, that organizations starting work today will require 10 years to reach that level. Fortunately, the pioneers have provided much learning that is now being used to lead the change process more efficiently and effectively.

Descriptively, organizations at the advanced stage have visibly committed leaders. Biases still exist but are dealt with fairly and quickly when they surface. Organizations at this level are recognized as "best places to work" by many diverse sources. Diversity has become an integral part of business and human resource planning and implementation processes. In these stages diversity truly means "all the ways in which we differ." Differences are viewed as potential assets, and conflict is seen as an agent of creation.

Motivation to Act

Addressing diversity is seen as critical for success in the global and diverse marketplace. A heterogeneous population of students, faculty, staff, or associates is viewed as necessary for success with patients, customers, clients, and consumers. Diversity is also recognized as adding value by enhancing creativity and innovation. Diversity work is done to add or affirm unity while enhancing quality. In these stages diversity is seen as a key to growth and competitiveness.

Appropriate Interventions

As with the middle stages, there are myriad appropriate actions at this level. In fact, many of the interventions used during the middle stages are also beneficial here. Below we discuss some additional actions.

Full Integration
In these stages diversity is fully integrated into all other appropriate initiatives. This includes, but is not limited to: quality, team building, reengineering, change management, and other educational and training initiatives (e.g., supervisory, managerial, communication, marketing, and sales). At this stage no one considers putting together a team that is not diverse. Diversity becomes a habit and homogeneity causes discomfort when the organization is tackling complex issues and tasks.

Diversity Education and Training for All

By this time every participant in the organization has at least been involved in awareness training. In advanced organizations most participants also will have engaged in education and training to develop skills. Skill-oriented training addresses specific diversity issues such as cross-functional teaming, intercultural marketing, race, gender, age, and disabilities. It is likely that basic work on style diversity (e.g., Myers–Briggs) was done in the earlier stages. More challenging work on issues such as sexual orientation occurs in these advanced stages. Education and training on issues like color, religion, and national origin are expanded around the globe.

Employee Resource Group Development

Networks and affinity groups continue to develop during these stages. They are supported and even endorsed by the organization. New groups may focus on age, military background, sexual orientation, and male issues. Increasingly, alliances, joint efforts, and partnerships emerge across networks. Affinity groups gain recognition as explicitly enhancing the performance of participants and the overall organization.

Diversity Resource Development and Renewal

By this time less use is being made of external diversity expertise. The internal capability is well developed and undergoing continuous renewal and expansion. Diversity work is increasingly being conducted by participants in the organization. It is no longer the exclusive province of those with "diversity" in their titles. Everyone can, and many do, contribute to diversity progress.

Performance-Diversity Link

In all stages of development diversity is explicitly a part of performance appraisals and evaluations. It is often tied to compensation, incentives, or other rewards. The organization often does internal research to examine the relationship between its diversity performance and overall business performance.

As this link becomes internalized, organizations may cease to reward diversity work directly and shift toward rewards based on overall performance. When this shift is successful, it indicates that members of the organization clearly understand the impact diversity has on performance and are now intrinsically, or internally, motivated.

Global and Local Linkages

At this juncture, every member of the organization has been educated regarding effective global relations and communication. Worldwide issues (e.g., gender, religion, color, style, language, disabilities, age, cross-functional teaming) are addressed within local contexts. A global mindset reflects the valuing of differences; the diversity mindset reflects a global perspective.

Outreach and Partnerships

Alliances and mutually beneficial relationships are built with other organizations: Businesses adopt schools. Adult organizations run youth programs. Child care and elder care are linked. Roles are reversed for a day to develop empathy.

Cafeteria-Style Benefits

Benefits are designed to fit a more diverse population. Flexibility and choice are emphasized. Equality, equity, and fairness have replaced the practice of providing identical benefits for all.

Win-Win

Individuals and organizations in the advanced stages of development use tactics and strategies based on mutual benefit. The goal is for all parties to win. As the number of diverse groups and individuals grows, the focus shifts to enlarging the pie, not cutting it into more pieces. The guiding philosophy is to unify diverse elements and win, rather than to divide and conquer.

A Shattered Ceiling

As organizations enter the advanced stages, glass ceilings may not be completely broken, but at least they are cracked. An engineer can lead a social service agency. A woman can direct a military group. An Asian can lead a multinational team. A poor person can serve on the board of a wealthy foundation. Finally, when organizations are fully into the advanced stages, the ceilings are shattered. Competence is now the criterion for leadership and promotion. Competence includes both technical or task-oriented skills and interpersonal or people-oriented skills.

SUGGESTIONS FOR ORGANIZATIONAL DEVELOPMENT

Ultimately, the diversity change process produces results when the organization visibly acts on its commitment to diversity. Following are actions the organization can take to support this initiative.

- When the goals and efforts of the teams and individuals in the corporation are in alignment, strong leadership and supportive systems will be able to move the entire organization forward.
- Management must lead by example. Most diversity work fails or stagnates because the organization's leaders do not visibly support the work. In organizations with effective processes, the leaders take the wheel and drive the process by modeling the values and behaviors they expect. Inappropriate behavior is followed by appropriate consequences. Management both adheres to and enforces practices and policies to ensure a healthy climate for diversity. Management creates a climate where feedback on appropriate and inappropriate behavior is the norm.[5]
- Examine the environment to ensure that all aspects are conducive to diversity. For example, take steps to ensure that new products meet the criteria for successful introduction to international and diverse markets. The blunders cited earlier in this book will not occur. Even more important, diversity will be leveraged for success.
- Expect and accept, but do not be deterred by, setbacks to the process. Identify what went wrong, change it, learn from it, and move on. See failures as opportunities for future growth and success.
- Benchmark other organizations. Learn about diversity from those corporations and organizations that have more experience with it. Examine their systems and identify what will work best for your organization. If, for example, your institution is just starting out in its diversity work and the culture is conservative and traditional, focus your

initial efforts on those traits. Target your efforts to the diversity issues that are most pertinent to your organization and its strategy for the future.

- Set a clear direction and establish a strong rationale for diversity work within your organization.

SUMMARY

- Like individuals and groups, organizations go through predictable stages of development.
- If the work at one stage of development is incomplete, sustained progress toward later stages will be impeded.
- Many of the leading models of diversity or pluralistic organizational development are used by diversity professionals to guide all phases of diversity work.
- The models show the following generic stages of development: early—exclusive, resistant; middle—reactive, proactive; advanced—transitional, inclusive and high performing.
- In the early stages, organizations are motivated to act by internal dissatisfaction, external attacks, and poor performance with clients, customers, or consumers. Effective actions during the early stages include: needs assessments, team building, business case development, identification of resources, and introductory awareness or compliance training.
- In the middle stages, motivation to act comes from legal compliance pressure, internal demand, raised internal expectations, bad public relations, exposure, and high turnover among particular groups. Effective actions include: putting an internal diversity leader in place, two-way communication, personal work by leaders, benchmarking, human resource system reviews, and linking diversity to other initiatives.
- In advanced stages, motivation to act stems from a desire to be a preferred provider of goods, services, or education. It also stems from a desire for high sustained

organizational performance. Actions during the advanced stages tend to be flexible, creative, and proactive. They usually involve at least the following: integration of diversity into all systems, education and training for all participants, issue-specific and skill-oriented education and training, growth and development of employee resource groups, global–local linkages.

NOTES

1. Ann M. Morrison, *The New Leaders: Guidelines on Leadership Diversity in America,* Jossey-Bass Publishers, San Francisco, 1992.
2. Nancy Adler, in W. Warner Burke and Leonard D. Goodstein, eds., *Trends and Issues in OD: Current Theory and Practice,* San Diego, Calif.: University Associates, 1980.
3. Bailey Jackson, Rita Hardiman, and Mark Chesler, *Racial Awareness Development in Organizations* (Amherst, MA: New Perspectives, 1981).
4. Monica Armour, Transcultural International, 1993.
5. "Champions of Diversity" (a videotape by Copeland Griggs Productions: San Francisco, 1990) shows senior executives demonstrating their personal leadership regarding diversity.

5

CHAPTER

Strategy Variations

The overall stages of development remain consistent, even though organizations appropriately address diversity in unique ways because of their differing cultures, styles, and patterns of development. Any approach or strategy should be tailored and custom designed, however, to meet the needs of the organization using it.

Here are some keys to tailoring and shaping diversity strategies:

- Tie the initiative to or align it with specific business needs.
- Continuously invite the input and support of those individuals most affected by the initiative.
- Elicit the support and guidance of external stakeholders such as customers and vendors.
- Continue to leverage and align with other organizational initiatives currently in place.
- Keep everyone informed about the progress of each initiative; give others ongoing opportunities to provide feedback needed to shape the work.

EFFICIENCY AND COST EFFECTIVENESS

As we look across employment sectors (e.g., nonprofit, education, government, private), or even within each sector, it is clear that the resources, that is, the time, money, and commitment available for diversity work vary greatly. Fewer resources mean that the work typically will take longer to make measurable progress. Aggressive diversity programs, on the other hand, are effective but often strive for a rate of change that is faster than participants can accommodate. Waste and loss of efficiency result.

Too much too fast means expending more energy on diversity than can be efficiently absorbed by the organization. But slow-paced pluralism initiatives can also be wasteful. Programmatic actions such as policy revisions, recruitment programs, and training should start within a few weeks of an initial needs assessment. When critical mass is not achieved quickly, repeated restarts will be required. Furthermore, failure to deliver promptly on commitments will necessitate stronger, more costly actions later to demonstrate sincerity.

While diversity initiatives positively impact productivity, profitability, and other measures of organizational performance, it normally takes at least 18–24 months for significant, measurable improvements to show up in large-scale performance. Organizations that terminate their diversity efforts after fewer than 18 months have probably quit within months of being able to see results.

Cost effectiveness and efficiency are enhanced when pluralism work is led by a professional with the requisite knowledge, skills, and abilities. The competencies needed by diversity professionals are outlined in Chapter 11, Diversity Competencies.

SELF-SUFFICIENCY

Most organizations today are working harder and smarter to achieve their objectives with as few resources as possible. To facilitate diversity work these organizations must either hire internal professionals with high skill levels in diversity or use external consultants to build and enhance their internal ability to deliver diversity services.

In recent years many major corporations, civic and professional organizations, units of government, and institutions of higher education have developed or hired highly capable internal diversity leaders.[1] Many organizations now explicitly tell consultants that their goal is self-sufficiency, with planned declines in the use of external expertise. For example, Ford, Pillsbury, Ryder System, and Deluxe Corporation make development of internal professionals an explicit part of their agreements with external consultants.

Organizations that do not plan for self-sufficiency often find themselves in the difficult position of having relied on external resources and funded only one or two phases of the work to be done. These organizations may discover that while progress has been made (if they have kept at the work for at least two years), the cost has been high. Simultaneously, they discover that the diversity program stalls whenever they stop using external consultants. At this crossroads the organization must continue to depend on consultants, hire competent internal professionals, or build in-house expertise by developing the skills of existing employees.

A large Midwestern newspaper found itself in this position in the early 1990s. The company had relied almost exclusively on external consultants to guide and conduct its diversity initiative. The initiative stalled and was not renewed until the mid-1990s, when the newspaper started developing more internal diversity leadership. In the lull of activity, morale within the company declined, primarily because of unmet expectations.

The combination of diversity skills and intimate knowledge of a company and its culture is powerful. In the long term, self-sufficiency is both more efficient and more effective. It not only reduces dependence on external resources, it also facilitates the institutionalization of change that is critical for sustained success. The most respected independent diversity consultants also emphasize the development and nurturing of internal talent.

BOTTOM-UP OR TOP-DOWN?

Which are the fastest and most effective ways to create a pluralistic, transformed organization? The flatter the organizational structure, the greater the impact of bottom-up, or grassroots, approaches. The more hierarchical the organization, on the other hand, the more likely it is that top-down, or management-driven, approaches will prove most effective.

Bottom-up approaches normally take two to three times as long as top-down approaches to create measurable change. Additional time is required to obtain resources and to stimulate change when organizational leaders are not driving the initiative. For maintaining momentum and sustaining change, bottom-up approaches tend to be more vulnerable to changes in management. However, bottom-up change tends to be more participative and more voluntary. Influence, persuasion, peer pressure, personal involvement, and spontaneity characterize this approach.

Top-down strategies are least effective when leaders fail to do as they tell others to do. Leading only by verbal guidance brings disappointment and cynicism. However, top-down approaches are highly effective when those at the top do enough personal diversity work to lead the change with deeds as well as words. Let's look at examples of both types of leadership in creating a strong diversity program.

A Bottom-Up Tale

Organization X began its diversity journey in the early 1970s. It started with a strong equal opportunity/affirmative action program led by competent professionals. As they examined human resource data—including organizational climate and employee attitudes—they decided that something more and different was needed to achieve their dual goal of increased profitability and recognition as a preferred employer.

The organization's values and ways of treating employees pointed the way forward. Its move toward what we now call diversity was organized as an alliance of equal opportunity, affirmative action, and a commitment to value variety among the workers. Beginning with middle-level employees and a few senior managers, the organization started what would later be called valuing-differences work.

This effort met most of the criteria that we use today to define excellence in diversity work. The definition of diversity included *all* differences, not just race and gender. Participants explored both their general ways of dealing with difference (e.g., stereotyping, making assumptions, building personal relationships, examining group and individual patterns) and their experiences in dealing with specific differences (e.g., race, gender, education, work). In all this exploration differences were valued, commonalities recognized, and unity emphasized.

Throughout this very large organization (more than 100,000 employees) the effort was well supported by human and fiscal resources alike. Virtually every employee took part in some type of diversity training. Diversity became an integral part of the organizational culture, and by the mid-1980s it was known around the world as a model of diversity excellence.

Yet though he allowed the work to continue throughout his tenure, Organization X's CEO never became a personal advocate. He never visibly engaged in personal diversity work. The program was successful, so it seemed, in spite of the absence of leadership from the top.

Then in the late 1980s and early 1990s the organization encountered challenging economic times. Major changes to meet the challenge included downsizing and many replacements among senior managers. The organization's reputation for excellence in diversity faded. As of 1996 it has not recovered. Although Organization X had been firmly into advanced stages of diversity work, it cycled back to the middle phases. It continues to move toward advanced stages today.

A Top-Down Tale

Company Y also began its diversity journey with equal opportunity and affirmative action programs, which proved sufficient to keep the company out of litigation for many years. The programs were staffed by professionals and had fiscal support, but senior management was little involved.

In the late 1980s the organization was acquired by another company. Many cost-reduction measures (including downsizing) were adopted, and all corporate initiatives were thoroughly reviewed.

The new management team shifted to a diversity focus while keeping equal opportunity and affirmative action as supportive policies and practices. This diversity effort met the criteria for excellence in terms of definitions, areas of emphasis, sequencing, and dedicated resources. The education and training initiative moved from team building and general diversity work to workshops on race, gender, style, sexual harassment, culture, age, cross-functional team building, disabilities, sexual orientation, and religion.

Senior executives participated first in this series of sessions. The CEO and management team took part in one-on-one and small group sessions. Once they had completed the series, managers, supervisors, and employees followed. Initial work was managed by an internal executive who oversaw the organizational process and contracted with consultants who helped with strategy and facilitated training.

By the early 1990s most of the work was being led and performed by internal people. By 1996 virtually every executive had participated in at least two or three sessions. Most employees also had attended the introduction to diversity and one or two issue-specific workshops. Many executives and employees had completed more than half a dozen sessions, some lasting as long as three days.

Between the late 1980s and 1996 Company Y also faced economic challenges and took strong cost-reduction and profit-enhancement measures. In spite of these events, the organization began receiving recognition as a "best place to work" in 1994. Its internal evaluations continue to show measurable improvement by almost every diversity indicator—program evaluations, representation, quality of work life, best practices, and more.

In 1994 Company Y was included in research to assess the relationship between diversity progress and financial performance in its industry. The research found a statistically significant relationship, which grew stronger as the period of analysis was extended from one to five to 10 years. This company was the top financial performer in the study, and it was in the top quartile regarding diversity. It had taken the company about five years to achieve that status. In 1996 Company Y was clearly entering the advanced stages of diversity work.

The Differences Between the Tales

Organization X, the organization in our bottom-up tale, was a pioneer ahead of its time. Much of what we know today about conducting effective diversity work was learned in this organization. The organization was also generous in sharing its expertise around the globe. Its primary failing was a lack of advocacy by senior executives. Most of them, including the CEO, did not visibly support the effort.

Company Y started much later and could tap a wider base of experience and knowledge as it began diversity change work. It also profited from the personal involvement and support of senior management, beginning with the CEO. By the early 1990s internal resource development enabled the organization to be highly self-sufficient. Skilled internal diversity leaders enabled the organization to sustain the effort while continuing to reduce direct expenditures for diversity initiatives.

Bottom-up approaches can work if given enough time and re-sources. Top-down is faster.

TOTAL INTEGRATION

Many organizations begin by saying they will integrate diversity into everything they do. When pressed about what they are going to integrate, they say "diversity." When asked, "What is diversity?" their answers are often vague.

Ultimately, diversity must indeed be integrated into all systems and activities. Before this can happen, however, diversity must be accepted, respected, and valued. Before diversity can be woven into business planning, non-diversity education, and all people-oriented processes, a foundation specific to diversity must be built.

This initial specific diversity focus must build awareness and skills regarding a wide range of diversity issues. Individuals must first understand what diversity is, how it impacts performance, and how to interact effectively with people who are different. The aim is to create a climate in which anyone who is different (which means *everyone*) feels accepted (at least), respected (preferably), and valued (ideally).

Only after this foundation has been built can integration occur, because there is something substantial to integrate.

Pilot Programs

Many companies begin their work with pilot initiatives in one or more parts of the organization. This strategy allows those parts that are ready to begin work—without waiting for others.

Multiple pilot programs can create a healthy climate of competition as well as provide some creative experimentation.

A good example of pilot strategy occurred in the Pillsbury Technology Organization. This part of the company piloted work that went beyond mere awareness and addressed more challenging diversity issues before the company as a whole took them on. After training that included general awareness, technology workers moved to issue-specific areas. They addressed style, race, gender, and sexual harassment in the first few years. In later years they went deeper into racial issues, added work on sexual orientation, and examined the implications of religious diversity. All the work focused on enhancing organizational performance.

Overall organizational goals should be common across the units engaged in pilot programs. Methods of achieving the goals may vary and should be custom designed for the style and culture of each organizational unit. For example, diversity efforts in technical organizations are likely to have many educational components, sophisticated measurements, informal mentoring, and significant emphasis on cultural and work-style differences. In sales organizations diversity efforts are more likely to have training components, quantitative measures, formal mentoring, and significant emphasis on differences reflected in the customer base. In short, the technical organization may have more of an internal emphasis while sales may be more externally focused.

TO MANDATE OR PERSUADE?

As organizations introduce diversity initiatives, the question often arises whether to require or to invite employees to take part.

Some requirements are clearly appropriate for every employee: All must know the inclusive definition of diversity. All must understand why diversity is important. All must recognize what types of behavior are appropriate or not with fellow workers different from themselves. Competence and common understanding are not optional in these areas.

However, all employees should have available a range of methods for gaining the mandated understanding and competence.

And exploration of emotions and feelings about diversity change should *not* be required.

Good organizations make certain that all participants know what diversity is and have clear guidelines for appropriate behavior. Better organizations add an understanding of why diversity is important and how it affects performance. The best organizations also support safe, professionally guided emotional work on diversity issues. This "heart work" has a major positive impact on the climate for everyone. It also enhances participants' individual effectiveness in all aspects of personal and professional life. While emotional work should not be required, it can be encouraged, made inviting, and rewarded. It must, however, be conducted by *professional* diversity facilitators.

Requiring individuals to attend training sessions is rarely the best strategy. Words like "invited," "encouraged," and "urged" should be prominent in announcements of training components in diversity initiatives. When this approach is taken, the attendance of invited individuals usually starts at about 75 percent and rises to 100 percent within a few sessions. The increase comes as soon as word spreads that the training did not hurt, was enjoyable, provided good insights, and was fun as well as educational.

By contrast, the learning climate is less healthy when participants come because "My boss said I had to." Effective facilitators often begin workshops by asking participants why they are in attendance. If attendance is mandatory or participants have been told they "need" training, facilitators must address their implicit concerns early.

The several steps a facilitator takes in such a situation are worth spelling out. They are listed below. Managers and other workers in diversity programs can use them, too.

- Listen carefully to each participant. Seek to ensure that all who are present feel they have been heard.
- Encourage all to share their feelings and attitudes about the session and the requirement to attend.
- Preview the workshop to allay people's fears of being excluded, becoming the focus of training, being accused of racism or sexism, or being made to feel guilty or emotionally abused.

- Let participants know that while they will not be forced to stay, disruptive behavior is not acceptable, and that in rare instances a participant may choose to or be asked to leave.

BEHAVIOR OR ATTITUDE: WHICH COMES FIRST?

Psychologists have debated this question for decades. The answer is "both or either."

Change can occur by first requiring different behavior. If you have to behave in a "new" way long enough, one of three things is likely to happen: (1) your attitude will change, as will your behavior; (2) you will leave the environment requiring the change; or (3) you'll suffer mental or emotional disturbance.

Behavior change can come quickly when rewards and disincentives reinforce healthy and discourage unhealthy behavior. The advantage of focusing on behavior is the speed of change. However, until there is concomitant attitude change, the new behavior is likely to be insincere.

Motorola's diversity initiative is a good example of strategy focused on behavior and results. Clear representation goals were set and results were carefully tracked. Motorola's reputation for achieving diversity at all levels is very good.

On the other side of the coin, doing the internal work required to change attitudes requires more time, repeated intervention, and permission to deal with feelings. Behavior may not change immediately, but change coming from within will bring the advantage of more genuine behavior. Further, attitude change affects a wide range of behaviors. Addressing attitudes on specific issues such as style, race, and gender can often be generalized to related issues such as culture, religion, and disability.

The diversity approach at Digital Equipment Corp. reflected an emphasis on attitude change. Much of the work involved education, training, and discussion groups designed to enhance personal growth and healthy attitudes regarding diversity.

The head–hand–heart image provides a simple framework for considering the difference between attitude and behavior. Organizations can *require* work involving the head and hand—knowledge, information, communication, problem solving, action. But they can only *invite* work involving the heart—one's feelings and emotions.

So which comes first? The short answer is this: Attitude change can lead to behavior change, and behavior change can lead to attitude change. The former is slower, less painful, and more enduring. The latter is faster, less comfortable, and subject to regression unless there is reinforcement. *Addressing any two of the three elements—head, hand and heart—will impact the third. We are strongest when all three can work together.*

For example, asking a person to move a car that has rolled onto a rock will likely bring an uncertain response about how it can be done. Asking a parent to move a car that has rolled onto his or her child produces an immediate confident action. In the former task, only the head and hand are engaged. In the latter task, head, hand, and heart are all engaged together.

INTERNAL EMPHASIS OR EXTERNAL?

Should pluralism initiatives focus on the diverse external market or on diversity inside the organization? The answer is "both," and the balance between the two will differ across organizations.

For example, in retail and sales organizations, individuals tend to work more independently. These organizations need to emphasize the external market and develop the abilities of internal diversity professionals to address that market. Organizations that put more emphasis on pluralism within typically have limited interaction with customers or consumers. Examples of internally focused functions and organizations are research, production, and distribution. Most organizations benefit from an emphasis on both internal participants and external clients, customers, or consumers.

FROM GENERAL TO SPECIFIC OR SPECIFIC TO GENERAL?

As mentioned in previous chapters, the most effective diversity initiatives are developmentally sequenced. Such sequencing enhances both efficiency and effectiveness.

Among professional diversity trainers there have now been decades of debate on how to sequence work that focuses on difference in general with work that addresses such specific issues as gender, age, race, and ethnicity. We recommend the following approach.

Build the Foundation First

Begin with a foundation-building workshop designed to deliver three messages and cover two areas of knowledge and awareness.

The Messages

The first message—to be communicated verbally, in writing, and experientially—is that diversity means "all the ways in which we differ," that is, culture, gender, style, background, and more. Differences are real and have significant impacts on how people interact. The use of the word "they" must decline, and the concept of "other" must go out of fashion. "Inclusion" must become a more actively applied concept.

The second message is that pluralism work is about differences *and* similarities. Similarities provide connections and facilitate relationships. Differences provide ingredients for synergy, innovation, and creativity.

The third message is that the goal is unity without uniformity (or unity with diversity). This key concept confirms the organization's shared objectives while encouraging participants to bring their own similarities and differences into play. Unity without uniformity affirms each person's uniqueness as an asset to contribute to overall organizational effectiveness.

Further, the message of unity without uniformity addresses people's fear that diversity is divisive and will lead to a fractured nation with multiple sets of rules. In fact, it points to achieving a truly united nation with a common set of rules by learning to value everyone's differences and developing the nation and its rules together.

Especially in the manufacturing sector, uniformity is frequently associated with quality. Against this background the meaning of uniformity in diversity-work contexts is sometimes misunderstood. Diversity and uniformity get cast as an either/or instead of as the both/and they truly are.

This contrast in meaning became especially apparent during a debate about quality and innovation at a large American automobile company. Leaders in the company reported that external authorities consistently gave the highest quality ratings to Japanese cars. At the same time they acknowledged that state-of-the-art technology was frequently developed in the United States, then perfected and mass produced abroad, to high quality standards. Standardized high-quality mass production may look like unity *with* uniformity. Diversity seems to be a different word.

But consider: Such production reflects uniformity of output, *not* uniformity of contributions to the output. Quality production comes from unity and clarity in vision, goals, and standards; uniformity of human inputs, on the other hand, limits creativity and innovation. Making improvements on an existing prototype requires precisely focused innovation. Developing new concepts for prototypes and products requires the creativity that diversity of inputs makes possible. A shared vision and unity around goals, combined with rich and diverse input, leads to innovation and high-quality products. The auto manufacturer with the highest combined "score" will excel in the market. In summary, the relationship between unity and diversity is more multiplicative than additive:

$$U \times D = E$$

Unity times Diversity equals Excellence.

Two Knowledge Components

The opening phase of a diversity program should also include well-presented information on the reasons to address diversity at all and on the fundamentals of pluralism work. First, because interests and motivations vary greatly, the program must provide a broad range of reasons for doing the work. Chapter 1, Rationales for Diversity Change, presents the case in depth for employees and for organizations. Here are seven specific areas to cover briefly in a foundation-building workshop:

1. Personal effectiveness.
2. Social and demographic changes (at work and in the market).
3. Litigation avoidance and resolution.
4. Employee and public relations.
5. Fairness, equity, ethics, and integrity.
6. Productivity (non-economic outputs).
7. Profitability (economic outputs).

A second knowledge component for early attention is a brief outline of the fundamentals of pluralism work. A reasonable and simple approach would be to summarize the Table of Contents of this book or other descriptive overview documents on personal and organizational diversity work.

Proceed to the Specifics Second

Once you have established a solid foundation, the training can then proceed to specific pluralism issues. For example, if the focus is cultural differences, work might begin with a general discussion of the dimensions along which cultures vary. It could then continue with explorations of specific cultures, but not in ways that reinforce stereotypes.

If race is the focus, work could begin by developing a common definition of racism, examining the ways in which racism gets started, identifying what sustains it, and discussing ways to reduce or eliminate it. The follow-up could be an in-depth exploration of racism against specific groups within and outside a nation's borders. This topic-specific work should examine the issues of original inhabitants as well as of those who came to the nation as immigrants, slaves, or indentured laborers. In short, while the phenomenon of racism is similar across groups, each group has a different history and presents unique contemporary dynamics. Both the generic similarities and the unique specifics should be explored.

Work on gender issues might start with an exploration of sexism, followed by attention to intra-gender issues as well as sexual orientation. As a large topic with a wide range of issues—gay, lesbian, bisexual, transsexual, transgender—sexual orientation may merit separate treatment. In any event, the pattern of examination must pay close attention to similarities as well as differences and avoid reinforcing stereotypes.

An excellent resource for the design of diversity training initiatives is the *Training and Development Handbook* (4th ed.), edited by Robert Craig (New York: McGraw-Hill, 1996).[2]

SUMMARY

- The diversity practices selected for implementation should fit the unique needs and culture of the organization.
- Diversity strategy requires alignment with other business needs, periodic monitoring, support from all stakeholders, and extensive communication and feedback.
- It typically takes at least 18–24 months before measurable, large-scale impacts are evident.
- Becoming self-sufficient by building internal capability is critical for cost effectiveness and continuity.
- Top-down approaches to diversity training work faster. Bottom-up approaches can be effective, but move more slowly and are more fragile.
- Diversity cannot be integrated into organizational systems until work has been done to build a diversity work foundation.
- Pilot programs are an excellent way to test approaches.
- Persuasion is better than mandating that individuals participate in diversity education and training.
- Directly addressing behavior quickly leads to visible change. Addressing attitudes produces slower but more durable change.
- The most effective diversity initiatives address knowledge, behavior, *and* attitudes.
- Comprehensive diversity initiatives address both the external customer and the internal participants in the organization.
- Diversity education and training should begin with a general foundation including the what, why, and how of diversity work. Issue-specific sessions should follow.
- U × D = E (Unity times Diversity equals Excellence).

NOTES

1. Among the major corporations that have developed or hired internal diversity leaders are: Ford, Pillsbury, Deluxe Corp., Hughes Aircraft, Norwest Bank, Amoco, Bank of Boston, Levi Strauss, Allstate Insurance, and American Express Financial Advisors. Among civic and professional organizations: American Society for Training and Development, Girl Scouts of America, YWCA, YMCA, United Way of Minneapolis, and National Conference of Christians and Jews. Among government entities: Hennepin County (Minn.), Internal Revenue Service, City of Austin, Tex., State of Oregon, and Province of Alberta. In higher education: Amsterdam Summer University (The Netherlands), Southern Illinois University, Texas A&M University, Dallas County Community College System (Tex.), and Oakland Community College (Mich.).

2. Robert L. Craig (editor in chief), *The ASTD Training & Development Handbook: A Guide to Human Resource Development*, 4th ed., McGraw-Hill, New York, 1996.

6

CHAPTER

Preparation

Factors to Consider

Many companies that launched diversity initiatives in the 1970s and 1980s overlooked factors that are now known to be crucial to the success of these efforts. Likewise, many well-known obstacles to human productivity are heavily influenced by diversity issues. Organizations seeking to launch or reenergize a diversity initiative can avoid many of these past mistakes and build on the extensive knowledge gained from three decades of experience.[1] This chapter covers the major obstacles and key overlooked factors, including communicating the vision, comprehensiveness and sequencing, developing competent internal resources, and environmental, systemic, and human factors.

COMMUNICATING THE VISION

The authors have discovered in their own work that many employees today do not know or do not understand the mission and vision of their organization, much less their own roles with respect to diversity. In particular, employees do not see how their individual work fits with the company's vision and contributes to its mission.

Organizations that successfully integrate and leverage diversity articulate their vision and mission to all of their members. A common way to foster clear articulation is for department heads to meet with workers to discuss the vision, define the mission, and highlight the ways that all department members contribute to achieving the company-wide goals and objectives. People want information, but many organizations do a poor job of providing information to their employees. Effective organizations are careful to communicate the "big picture" to their workers without watering down the message or condescending to their listeners.

Employees are less threatened by diversity initiatives when they see how such initiatives fit into their company's goals and objectives. An effective vision statement describes how the organization's leaders hope to use diversity principles to meet organizational goals. Organizations that move beyond traditional diversity approaches have leaders who set a clear direction for the process.

Incorporating diversity into an organization's vision statement accomplishes the following:

- Ensures the long-term success of diversity initiatives.
- Positions diversity as a viable tool to accomplish organizational objectives.
- Enables the organization to leverage diversity to maximize value for all stakeholders.
- Helps translate the vision into measurable results.

Born out of its vision and mission, the values of an organization are also critical pieces of the diversity process. Diversity work is a vehicle to translate values into observable and measurable processes and outcomes. Because employees compare the organization's behavior to its values, rhetoric, alignment of values and actions is critical to the credibility of any diversity initiative.

For example, a well-established, mid-sized international food company located in the U.S. sought to improve its performance. It downsized, sold poorly performing assets, reengineered, shifted from functional groups to cross-functional teams, improved the link between compensation and company performance, and initiated diversity work. These actions all occurred in a five-year period. In year three, the company implemented a comprehensive communication effort to make sure everyone understood its vision and mission.

Face-to-face meetings, videotapes, audiotapes, prominently posted written materials, and reminders in newsletters were used to communicate the vision and mission to all of the company's employees. Indicators of measurable progress toward mission accomplishment were developed and tracked. People and diversity were noted as critical to realize the vision and accomplish the mission.

With all of these communication vehicles in place, years four and five were record-breaking. The company enjoyed improvements in quality of work life, as well as significantly better financial performance. The company was recognized as a "preferred employer" and reported the strongest earnings in its industry peer group. While no single action accounted for these results, valuing diversity no doubt facilitated the creativity and innovation necessary for exceptional success in the marketplace. The clarity of vision and mission provided the unity the company needed to achieve quality while accomplishing defined objectives.

THE IMPORTANCE OF COMPREHENSIVENESS AND SEQUENCING

Comprehensiveness makes diversity work viable and sustainable. Developmental sequencing contributes to both its efficiency and effectiveness. The models of individual, group, and organizational development described in Chapters 3 and 4 help guide appropriate sequencing. Together, comprehensiveness and sequencing produce the desired results.

By contrast, poorly sequenced and single-faceted initiatives are costly and prone to failure. By their nature, such programs tend to be short-lived. This is because they focus on objectives and tactics rather than goals and visions, are not systemic in nature, and are rarely integrated with an organization's core processes.

Comprehensiveness

Choice of words is important for clear communication. In this book we choose such terms as *initiative, work, process, change, operation,* and *function* to go with *diversity.* "Diversity work," for example, conveys the comprehensive, pervasive nature of diversity itself. On the other hand, "diversity program" or "diversity project," though sometimes appropriate, suggest discrete actions, limited, even temporary. To be successful, the diversity process must be comprehensive.

A large international corporation (300,000 employees, annual sales more than $100 billion) initiated its diversity effort by assigning responsibility to the training department. As is often the case, the first step was a training program to introduce diversity. However, the program was designed by education and training professionals who had limited diversity expertise. Understandably, they designed the program as they would other educational programs in the company. But diversity work is not "another educational program." Treating it as such led to several serious mistakes, including the following:

- Program design began without a needs assessment.
- Implementation of the training was made mandatory for all managers and supervisors.
- Delivery agents were mandates, not volunteers.
- Senior executives did not participate in the program first.
- An appropriate context for the effort (diversity vision, mission, and leadership endorsement) was missing.
- There were no linkages to other human resource and business programs or processes.

As a result, the initial diversity effort failed. The training stopped after a few unsuccessful sessions. In most organizations that would have been the end of the story.

Fortunately, this organization had resources and advocates in other parts of the company. The initiative was relaunched in accordance with state-of-the-art models for diversity work. As of 1996, the company was in the middle stages of diversity development and on a course toward entering the advanced phases.

It is easy to terminate and difficult to recover from the early failures of a diversity program that is created in isolation. When the effort is more comprehensive, however, difficulty in one or even several areas (recruitment, policy development, mentoring, training, succession planning, equity programs) does not automatically condemn the entire effort to failure. Similarly, when cost reductions and downsizing are required, isolated activities are at risk of elimination. When diversity is a small but integral part of the work of many participants, it is very difficult to eliminate the diversity initiative without also destroying other vital functions.

This systemic, comprehensive approach also creates natural synergies with work being done by many members of the organization. Thus, effective and efficient diversity strategies typically include:

- A small number of internal people who are fully dedicated to lead diversity work.
- Selected external expertise.
- A large number of internal people who each make small, ongoing contributions.

Sequencing

Developmental sequencing is also critical in diversity work. Progress occurs fastest when the process begins with accurate diagnoses (including needs assessment and issue identification) at the individual, group, and organizational levels. Diagnoses enable diversity professionals to start at the "right" place instead of with programs suited for a stage that has already been passed or not yet been reached. The former is wasteful; the latter is ineffective, will be poorly received, and creates a need for remedial work later.

Readily available developmental models and knowledge gained by pioneers in the field make it possible for some organizations to accomplish in five years what organizations in the 1970s and 1980s needed 10 or 15 years to finish.

Developmental models move diversity work from an art toward a science.

COMPETENT INTERNAL RESOURCES

For the best combination of efficiency and effectiveness, organizations need to develop or hire internal diversity professionals. Five arguments support this opinion. Discussion of each point follows.

Internal Resources Understand Context, Culture, and Style

While external professionals can learn about an organization's context, culture, and style, doing so takes both time and financial support. Individuals who are strong contributors to an institution already possess this understanding. Knowledge of these aspects is critical in shaping an initiative to fit each unique unit and organization. Ignoring the context, violating cultural norms, or exhibiting an unacceptable style can disable an otherwise competent person.

Internal Resources Cost Less

External consulting rates typically exceed the hourly costs for internal members of organizations—true even when both direct and indirect internal costs are counted. In addition, consultants often come from distant locations and incur expenses for transportation and living expenses away from home.

In the mid-1990s most recognized diversity expertise still resides with external consultants, however. Once management makes an active commitment to diversity work, resources to get started usually become available. But if internal expertise is not developed or hired in the first year or soon thereafter, the initiative may stall as management begins to see the escalating cost of using consultants. At this point internal professionals often become an absolute necessity. It is even better to supplement a general internal expert with staff members who each have a few, specific diversity competencies.

Internal Consultants Provide High-Quality Services

While incompetent external diversity consultants do exist, many excellent consultants are available. A recent comparison between highly rated external consultants and in-house adjunct agents (people with other roles who spend a small percentage of their time on diversity work) reinforces the point.

The study compared evaluation sheets from introductory diversity workshops. Evaluations from sessions led by internal adjunct agents were compared to those from sessions led by external experts. On a five-point scale (where 1 = poor, 5 = outstanding), the external consultants averaged about 4.6. There were very few scores below 4.0 or above 4.7. Internal facilitators averaged about 3.9, with few scores falling below 3.6 or above 4.5. The small quantitative difference in favor of external experts goes along with a significantly higher cost. Internal agents produced high quality at lower costs.

Open-ended evaluations in a similar comparison clearly acknowledged the high level of subject-matter expertise possessed by external consultants, but occasionally noted difficulties in translating the outsiders' concepts for use by those who took part in the training. Open-ended evaluations about internal facilitators were also positive overall and frequently included comments like: "It was a good workshop, and the fact that the facilitator was one of us made it better."

Internal Resources Assure Timely Action

In addition to travel and per diem expenses, external consultants must usually be scheduled well in advance. If services are needed on short notice or extremely flexible scheduling is required, internal professionals have a large advantage. Most consultants charge fees for canceled work; most in-house professionals do not. In addition, communication by phone or e-mail, and one-on-one or group meetings is typically easier among internal members.

Internal Resources Provide Continuity

Lasting organizational change requires sustained advocacy, competent leadership, and institutionalization of new processes. Internal professionals are more likely than external consultants to engage in the formal and informal efforts needed to keep initiatives alive. They are also more likely to understand the politics that drive and restrain progress in any organization. Internal diversity workers have the advantage of continuing to contribute to the overall diversity vision even though they may move to different positions or roles in the organization. They remain in the pool of diversity resources wherever they reside.[2]

With respect to expertise, diversity work is a little like medicine: General practitioners inside the organization periodically find that they need to consult outside specialists in order to address a particular challenge or opportunity. The specialists are often external consultants with in-depth expertise in certain areas or additional experience working with certain issues.

Both internal and external diversity professionals are necessary for success. Ongoing and ultimate diversity leadership must be internal.

DON'T FOCUS ON GENDER AND RACE FIRST

Because gender and race are two significant ways in which we differ, diversity work must, of course, address these issues. Effective programs, however, start by discussing inclusive definitions of diversity that go beyond gender and race. From the start they encompass a wide range of other issues, too.

In so doing, some participants, especially women and people of color, are often heard to object, "This is a waste of our time," or "You're letting white males off the hook. When are you going to deal with real issues?" If diversity leaders yield to this pressure and focus initially on race and/or gender, resistance and backlash to the process will likely increase, not decrease. An early focus on these specific issues violates an inclusive definition of diversity. It also brings up old baggage associated with poorly implemented affirmative action and confrontational or abusive training experiences. Further progress is bound to be impeded.

Nevertheless, the feelings expressed by potentially dissatisfied groups of participants must be acknowledged and respected. Once the pain associated with their perspectives has been recognized, diversity leaders can explain that an inclusive approach eventually produces much greater attention to gender and race than one which begins with these issues.

Diversity work must include a commitment to fully address issues of race, gender, and other important ways in which people differ (e.g., styles, disabilities, age, functions, disciplines, roles, or sexual orientations).[3]

LEADERSHIP AND MANAGEMENT PRACTICES

It would be easy but absurd to blame all diversity problems on ineffective management and leadership practices. In the real world, managers manage and leaders lead with many more challenges than diversity on their minds. The discussion in this segment keeps that complexity in view, while recognizing that people do tend to feel that the way they are managed has everything to do with their feelings of self-worth and overall level of performance. There is no doubt that leadership and management practices directly impact employees.

Consider the following scenario: During a presentation to a group of senior managers, the managers debated ways to move their company's diversity process forward. During the discussion, a senior vice president disagreed with the CEO on a particular point. The CEO bluntly told the vice president that things would be the CEO's way. The vice president acquiesced, but pointed out that sharing different points of view is what diversity is all about. Significantly, the CEO recognized his error and apologized. The group went on to discuss the point further and arrived at a new solution that reflected the opinions of the group, the vice president, and the CEO.

This story illustrates the impact one person's behavior can have on the behavior and reactions of others. The authors have observed many similar situations in which leaders and managers have wanted things done their way and have failed to encourage—or even allow—other perspectives and opinions. Such behavior adversely impacts other employees' sense of self-worth and, ultimately, their overall performance.

Fortunately, innovative leaders and managers have numerous ways available to them to create a more inclusive environment. Many begin with a self-assessment against such factors as how they relate to people, how they manage their time, and where they place their energy and focus. They actively seek feedback and are open to other perspectives on their knowledge, attitudes, and behavior. As they continuously strive to understand how others perceive them and how they perceive themselves, they effectively determine when, how, and why they wish to modify their behavior.

Self-assessment also helps identify the work-related factors that most influence a manager's behavior. Many managers feel constant pressure to "get results"—especially results that explicitly improve the bottom line. This pressure can seriously interfere with a manager's ability to "tune in" to the human needs of others. It robs time and energy from people management, which is also critical to bottom-line results.

Other managers find their behavior heavily influenced by the culture of their organization. Conservative, traditional organizations tend to encourage and reward task-oriented, hierarchical management. This focus fosters territorialism and turf conflict while diverting attention from the development of strong communication and people skills.

It is imperative that organizations encourage leaders and managers to assess their behavior periodically, modifying management and leadership practices to ensure they are appropriate for diverse members and markets. As Max De Pree, former CEO of Herman Miller, Inc., stated in his book, *Leadership is an Art*, "*When we think about leaders and the variety of gifts people bring to corporations and institutions, we see that the art of leadership lies in polishing and liberating and enabling those gifts.*"[4]

ENVIRONMENTAL FACTORS

As organizations begin to examine their diversity efforts, they typically encounter a key question: "What does an environment that values diversity really look like?" In such an environment employees might answer that they:

- Like coming to work, feel comfortable at work, and enjoy their day-to-day interactions with co-workers.
- Feel accepted and respected by their managers and peers.
- Feel challenged and energetic.
- Feel appropriately recognized and rewarded for their contributions.

The actions and behaviors of people in the organization clearly indicate whether the environment successfully manages and values diversity. Organizational assessments conducted early in the diversity process can help identify discrepancies between stated organizational values and workplace behavior. "Profiles in Change," a videotape by Copeland Griggs Productions (San Francisco, 1990) gives an excellent visual and auditory description of real organizations successfully creating healthy environments.

When attempting to create or maintain such an environment, organizations cannot overlook or minimize the ongoing impact of changes that buffet today's institutions. Factors like rightsizing, reductions in force, enrollment declines, mergers, reengineering, and empowerment initiatives significantly influence employee attitudes and behaviors. Some of those attitudes and behaviors translate into diversity issues and concerns.

When organizations cut their workforce, for example, there is always a risk that one or more groups will be disproportionately impacted. In the 1990s this means that employees who are older, female, immigrants, and/or people of color often face a higher risk of being laid off, whether for lack of seniority, perceived weaker performance, or plain discrimination.

Cultural differences affect organizational mergers, acquisitions, and other change initiatives. When a company from one nation acquires or merges with a company that has a different national culture, conflict is inevitable. The conflict is often grounded in differing cultural views about people and profits. A dominant focus on pure productivity, without attention to such cultural or societal values as full employment, respect for elders, and seniority, can derail well-intended reengineering efforts. Likewise, attempts to foster empowerment may meet with resistance from employees who, for reasons of culture or personality, prefer and expect managers to make most decisions.

Such environmental factors have the greatest negative impact on employees in an organizational culture that is monocultural, exclusive, overly authoritarian, and risk-averse. It is ironic that some organizations which adhere to these approaches have vision and mission statements reflecting the value they place on customers, internal human resources, creativity, and innovation.

SYSTEMIC FACTORS

An organization's policies and systems can be obstacles or supports to its diversity initiative. Before launching a diversity initiative, an organization should audit its systems and policies to ensure that they are supportive of a diverse workforce and customer base. Do they reflect the needs and expectations of diverse customers and employees? Are they managed, administered, sold, marketed, educated, and served in a manner consistent with diverse needs and values?

Research conducted by the authors points to five human resource systems that are most likely to impact effective management of diverse employees. These are: communication, benefits, recruitment, rewards and recognition, and performance management.

Communication

Communication, or the lack it, is one of the most cited examples of barriers to effective diversity management. As we said earlier in this chapter, employees frequently feel they are not given enough information or do not have access to the information they need in order to contribute fully to organizational goals and objectives. This situation is exacerbated in organizations that lag behind technologically.

Employees want management to see them as capable, intelligent professionals who can handle information. Enhanced communication is a vehicle that gives employees the information and direction they need to contribute fully.

Effective communication plans include strategies for sharing long- and short-term business goals and for specifically addressing issues uncovered through climate surveys or needs assessments.

Benefits

Organizations that do not have competitive benefits find it increasingly difficult to attract capable employees. The benefits offered by an organization must be appropriate for a diverse population and flexible enough to adapt to changing needs over the lifetimes of individual employees. Such benefits are best presented "cafeteria style," with user-friendly guidance in decision making. "Cafeteria style" typically means giving employees an allotment of money that can be distributed across many benefit choices in order to fit each unique employee situation.

As is true with many diversity work issues, specific developmental sequences describe the evolution of benefit plans. Child care eventually progresses to dependent care. Maternity leave eventually becomes parental leave and adoption benefits are added. Parental leave evolves into personal leave. Part-time and flex-time become flexible work arrangements that encompass work hours, work places, and work styles. Insurance and retirement benefits extend coverage beyond the bounds of the traditional family. Parents, grandparents, partners, companions, and extended-family members are included. On-the-job education expands from instruction offered to the employee at the work site to a wide range of options involving technology and alternative educational institutions. Education benefits are eventually extended to cover extended-family members.

The cafeteria approach allows the organization to limit costs while offering its members choice and flexibility. Equity is achieved without providing identical benefits for everyone. Excellence in the provision of benefits has been shown by DuPont, St. Paul Companies, and U.S. West.

Recruitment

Traditionally, recruitment has been a standard element of most diversity initiatives, with efforts typically directed at women and people of color. Sometimes recruitment efforts are extended to include people with disabilities or older people.

Even when the focus is limited to people of color and women, successful recruitment and retention of employees from these groups correlates significantly with increases in stock market prices. As noted in Chapter 1, after four years of diversity work companies successful in this arena enjoyed stock prices some 10 percent higher than other organizations.

Recruitment practices in most organizations move through a seven-stage developmental sequence.

The Exclusive Club

The first stage is essentially an exclusive club arrangement—no one need apply who fails to fit explicit qualifications and demographic parameters. For example, "We need a new sales manager. We are looking for a middle-aged family man who can travel about 50 percent of the time."

Equal Opportunity

Second comes an equal opportunity approach. At this juncture there are no explicit demographic limitations—anyone meeting the entrance, admission, or job requirements can compete for an opportunity.

Enhanced Equal Opportunity

Enhanced equal opportunity comes next. Special programs provide support to help members of underrepresented groups compete for potential opportunities. Scholarships, intern programs, and other initiatives enlarge the pool of applicants for positions. Once pre-competition support is completed, all candidates are considered equally.

Some employers in this stage remove all demographic data from materials used to select among candidates. The aim is to achieve a color-blind, gender-blind, age-blind process. Even résumé items that give away demographic specifics (e.g., membership in an association of Asian engineers, a society of women physicians, or a senior citizens' council), may be deleted for the sake of "blind" consideration.

Soft Affirmative Action

The fourth stage, soft affirmative action, includes proactive efforts to get underrepresented groups on the candidate list. The focus tends to remain on groups covered by equal-opportunity protection. Advertising includes such outreach messages as, "Women and minorities are encouraged to apply." Final selection continues to be based on competencies, without consideration of demographic or other background characteristics.

Hard Affirmative Action

Hard affirmative action, distinguishable from soft at the point of selection, is the fifth recruitment stage. If a candidate from an underrepresented group is equally qualified with other top candidates, that person is proactively chosen. The emphasis at this stage is on qualifications; poorly qualified applicants are not selected.

Proactive Diversity Recruitment

The sixth stage is proactive diversity recruitment, at which point employers seek out all underrepresented types of diversity that might contribute to organizational effectiveness. Diverse slates of highly qualified candidates are consistently prepared as vacancies occur. The aim is to choose the candidate most likely to enhance overall team and organizational performance. While this might not be the person with the best skill score, it is never one who lacks highly developed technical ability. The overriding criterion is who will add the most value, not who is the highest individual achiever.

Unlike the previous stages, this stage considers *all* relevant differences. It is likely to mean, for example, adding sales expertise to the marketing team, production knowledge to the development staff, sociological perspectives to the psychology department, an understanding of face-to-face service delivery to social service agency management, women to all-male teams, Americans to all-European groups, and people of color to all-white organizations.

Inclusion and Transformation
The seventh developmental recruitment stage is inclusion and transformation. This final stage is reached when diversity is present, accepted, and respected. The emphasis here is on making diversity a natural and valued feature of the institution. Diversity work produces continuous personal growth and enhances organizational performance.

Advanced development in the area of recruitment means seeking diversity and recognizing the value it adds.

Rewards and Recognition

Diversity change implies diversity-focused rewards and recognition along with an employer's more general reward and recognition system. Positive feedback specifically pertaining to diversity change is needed early in any diversity effort.

Some organizations link managerial pay to diversity actions and results. Specific actions (e.g., participation in training, mentoring, supporting employee resource groups) and measurable results (e.g., improved hiring and retention, positive employee attitudes, reduction in litigation costs) are rewarded as part of a bonus payment or considered when making salary adjustments. The best incentive systems evolve from those that reward for activities and results to ones that reward primarily results.[5]

Ultimately, the diversity aspect of appraisal and recognition becomes more implicit and is integrated into the overall appraisal and reward systems. Diversity-specific rewards become unnecessary as managers recognize that diversity adds value. They then value diversity as a means of achieving organizational results. Diversity becomes intrinsically valued.

Equity of application is a potential diversity issue in overall reward and recognition systems. People will notice and (rightly) be offended if members of some groups get a disproportionate share of rewards in the organization—technical professionals, for example, or salespeople, younger employees, men, headquarters staff, tenured faculty members, political appointees. Rewards and recognition *must* be given only when deserved. Diversity is not a criterion for the distribution of awards. However, if members of particular groups are rarely recognized, the organization must review its recognition process to ensure that it is free of prejudice and bias.

Performance Management

Internal diversity professionals often see performance management as a problem area. Difficulties frequently surface when a supervisor is about to give negative performance feedback to someone who is different. The manager often fears being accused of bias or prejudice. When this fear arises, the supervisor seeks assistance from the diversity professional before proceeding. This is an especially common scenario in the middle stages of diversity development.

In earlier stages of diversity change, the poor performer probably would not have received any significant corrective feedback at all. From the 1970s to the early 1990s many supervisors were reluctant to be critical of employees covered under civil rights legislation—indeed, supervisors still may be when diversity initiatives have just begun. But as global competition increases performance pressure, performance discussions become more candid. And when diversity is involved, these discussions may be even more difficult, and surprised recipients of negative feedback are likely to go to diversity professionals for assistance or to protest.

Informally generated internal complaints, formal complaints, and litigation often stem from incidents involving performance management. However, in the later stages of diversity development, constructive performance feedback increases and is a major stimulus to improved individual and organizational performance. This feedback unlocks the performance potential of both the recipients and givers.

Learning to manage performance of diverse individuals is an essential supervisory skill.

Task Systems

In addition to examining people systems, diversity work also must address an organization's task systems. The functional systems most likely to affect performance in the diverse and global marketplace are all the systems in the product or service pipeline. Remember, diversity is *all* the ways in which we differ. Therefore, failure to value and leverage cross-functional diversity as part of conceptualization, development, production, marketing, educating, selling, servicing, recycling, and disposal leads to less competitive performance. Failure to value and leverage *all* the ways in which humans differ blocks creativity and innovation. As noted in Chapter 1, it also leads to missed opportunities and marketplace blunders.

HUMAN FACTORS

Every individual possesses a unique cultural perspective which influences his or her view of the world. To develop an effective partnership with the organization, individuals must do ongoing self-assessment work. Individuals cannot support and assist in the creation of an environment that accepts, respects, and values diversity if they are unclear about their personal values and perspectives.

The following are just some of the factors that affect each individual employee's commitment to diversity and the extent to which he or she contributes to the creation of a healthy working environment:

- Recognition and acceptance that diversity is not about any single group; its overriding goal is for *all* employees to feel included.
- The individual's capacity for tolerance, patience, tenacity, and determination.

- His or her personal ambitions, needs, and expectations.
- The individual's willingness to take personal responsibility for supporting and affecting change.

In addition, organizations on the verge of launching or re-launching diversity efforts should keep five human factors–related rules in mind during planning and preparation. These are discussed below.

Rule 1: Expect the Process to Be Long and Slippery

Many companies expect diversity efforts to bear fruit immediately after planting the first seeds of commitment via awareness training and other introductory activities. Yet even in the most expertly led and well-resourced initiatives, it usually takes at least 18–24 months before significant measurable progress occurs. There are excellent models to follow but there is no cookbook approach to diversity management; most efforts are characterized by at least a few periods of trial and error. A helpful thought to carry forward is that mistakes produce learning opportunities. Competent diversity professionals (see Chapter 11, Diversity Competencies) can shorten and smooth the process.

This caution is especially true for organizations that are leaders in diversity. These organizations face new situations without the benefit of having seen other organizations deal with similar situations. For example, U.S. West has a reputation for excellence with its eight employee resource groups (covering disabilities, race and ethnicity, women, and veterans). Early on, the company had to address such novel questions as whether to have a white male network, how to reenergize mature resource groups, synergies across groups, and appropriate levels of support.

Rule 2: Link Diversity Change to Key Organization Strategies

The results of diversity efforts hinge on how well the interventions are tied to key business objectives such as profitability, enrollment growth, sales, quality, productivity, service delivery effectiveness, human resource management, and the like. For example, a good part of Avon's diversity initiative was a direct link between re-cruiting and retaining more professionals of color and its strate-gies for gaining market share among customers of color. The strategies were successful, with measurable impact on Avon's fi-nancial performance.

Rule 3: Design the Diversity Process to Be Flexible and Responsive to Changes in the Environment

Every organization is unique. As such, the diversity issues faced by organizations can vary significantly. The same holds true for divisions, agencies, and departments within an organization. Clearly, the diversity process should take into account the unique needs and expectations of each unit.

The strategies used by individual units, however, must be aligned with the organization's overall diversity approach. Align-ment allows organizations to manage the process effectively and to leverage the key outcomes and results from one intervention to those being applied in other areas. When diversity growth is linked to business goals, business leaders are usually more assertive in pro-viding support for diversity work. In The Pillsbury Company, for ex-ample, most diversity work is funded directly by business leaders.

Rule 4: Design Process Management Tools to Focus on Results

As we discussed in Chapter 4, a new diversity effort should begin with a well-designed baseline assessment (as discussed in Chapter 4). The assessment may include several data-gathering methods, such as focus groups, one-on-one interviews, surveys, and other types of audits.

A planning table (see Figure 6–1) can be especially helpful in identifying and managing strategic diversity fundamentals.

Rule 5: Hold Individuals Accountable for Specific Strategies, Processes, and Interventions

Senior executives and diversity leaders in companies such as Ford and Pillsbury have explicit responsibilities for diversity in their

FIGURE 6–1

Strategic Diversity Planning Table

Diversity dimension	Opportunity Area	Strategy	Responsible Party	Indicator	Goal
White-male workforce	Perceived reverse discrimination	Communication regarding business rationale for diversity	Diversity task force senior managment	White males in diversity events and process	White male buy-in on diversity work
Systems Retention	Diversity at management levels	Minority recruiters mentor program	Directors Recruiters	More managers of color	x % increase by 1998
Exernal market Call-center customers	Insensitivity to "different" or "foreign" customers	Multilingual customer service reps	Call-center managers HR dept.	Fewer customer complaints	Provide excellent customer service
Structures Sales & marketing	No input from sales to marketing plan	Integrated sales & marketing planning task force	Sales and marketing managers	Sales supports marketing plan as effective	Integrated sales & marketing plan
Global Foreign parent company Foreign management	Clash of national cultures	Training Cultural awareness and skills	Training department Department managers	Less conflict between U.S. & foreign managers	Mutual appreciation of differing values, perspectives, beliefs, business practices

goals and objectives. The "owner" or sponsor of a specific diversity effort should ensure that:

- The effort ties to a specific organizational objective.
- It is linked to other initiatives such as quality, empowerment, reengineering. (See Figure 6–2.)
- Everyone understands the nature of the effort and the intended outcomes.
- Everyone is kept informed of the status and progress of the effort.
- The implementation of the initiative is documented.
- Critical milestones and checkpoints are identified.
- The process is monitored and evaluation criteria are regularly applied.

FIGURE 6–2

Diversity Dimensions: The Diversity Continuum

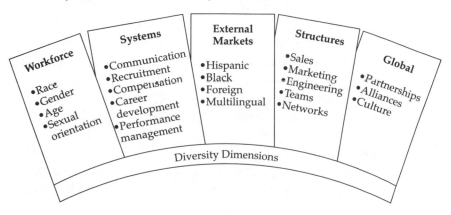

SUMMARY

- Frequent oversights in preparing for diversity work include the absence of a vision regarding diversity and communication of that vision, lack of comprehensiveness, and failure to sequence the work in a developmental fashion.

- Additional oversights involve failures to integrate diversity work with other organizational initiatives and develop sufficient internal diversity expertise.

- Successful integration of diversity requires that the organization articulate its mission and vision to all of its members.

- Comprehensiveness and proper developmental sequencing make diversity work sustainable and effective.

- Internal diversity resources help fit the approach to the context, minimize costs, maintain quality, assure timely action, and maintain continuity.

- A significant mistake in diversity work is addressing the specific topics of race and gender without first discussing inclusive definitions of diversity.

- An environment in which people do not feel valued or respected is an obstacle to progress.

- Systemic factors that must be addressed in preparation for a diversity initiative are the organization's policies and practices in communications, benefits, recruitment, rewards and recognition, performance management, and task systems.
- The diversity process must be applied to human resources and task systems such as product development, marketing, service delivery, selling, educating, and recycling.
- Leaders and managers must competently relate to people, manage time, and allocate sufficient energy and focus to people-oriented goals.
- Human factors also must be considered. They include dealing with recognition, acceptance, feelings of inclusion or exclusion, individual needs, and such personal qualities as tolerance and patience.
- Five rules provide insights into the diversity change. The process: (1) will be long and slippery; (2) must be linked to the organization's key strategies; (3) must be flexible and responsive to changes in the environment; (4) must focus on results; and (5) requires that individuals have specific responsibilities and be held accountable.

NOTES

1. Companies that have done diversity work for years are often generous in sharing their learning. Deserving special mention are DuPont, Ford, Digital Equipment, Pillsbury, American Express Financial Advisors, and Hughes Aircraft.
2. Good examples (from a rapidly growing pool) of internal diversity professionals reflecting these arguments are Romeo McNairy (Ford), David Barclay (Hughes Aircraft), Richard Gaskin (American Express Financial Advisors), Curtis White (Honeywell), May Snowden (U.S. West), and Kim Cromwell (Bank of Boston).
3. For a more extensive discussion of this issue, see V. Robert Hayles, "Accept, Respect, Value," Colors 3, no. 5 (1994), pp. 27–31.
4. Max De Pree, Leadership is an Art (Doubleday, 1989), p. 8. Several parts of this book are devoted to diversity.
5. A few examples of companies with strong diversity incentives are Tenneco, Hoechst, Celanese, Marriott International, and Deloitte & Touche.

7

The Road to Results

Conventional wisdom would have us believe that diversity initiatives, like many other human resource efforts, are hard to measure. But diversity does provide measurable significant outcomes for organizations. When implemented effectively, diversity processes enhance other initiatives and help the organization achieve its strategic objectives.

In this chapter we will discuss why diversity change measurement is important, the key requirements of implementation for good measurement, and six areas of measurement that should be developed.

KEY REQUIREMENTS

Effective implementation of diversity work has several key requirements that underlie good measurement of its results.

The first is to identify the business objectives that are directly impacted by diversity issues and tie accomplishment of those objectives back to the organization's vision statement. Three very different companies illustrate this point:

- Avon's success in expanding its market share in U.S. ethnic markets was directly attributable to its proactive recruitment and retention of sales and marketing professionals with intimate knowledge of the desired consumer communities.

- Pillsbury's successful entry into specific Hispanic markets followed proactive hiring and development of individuals with the needed language and cultural skills.
- International Distillers and Vintners increased its sales in Florida by understanding the diversity among its Spanish-speaking consumers.

A second requirement of good measurement is to identify the developmental gaps that have the greatest impact on employee productivity and ability to contribute to organizational goals. Third, good diversity initiatives make all employees responsible and accountable for diversity management. Fourth, there must be a clear plan to monitor and control the diversity process through periodic measurement and evaluation designed to assess results and provide useful feedback for modification and adaptation as the work moves forward.

MEASURING DIVERSITY CHANGE

Measurement is important for several reasons. In many organizations what does not get measured does not matter. Further, doubters and supporters alike need tangible evidence to be sure of progress. Unfortunately, informal, intuitive, and subjective measures, though valuable and useful, are often not persuasive as a basis for continuing budget support. Finally, as mentioned above, good measurements are vital to the ongoing refinement and adjustment that make any process effective and efficient.

It is important to obtain baseline measures at the outset of any diversity initiative. Baseline measures define the starting point of the effort and serve as a reference for other organizations while also pointing to further opportunities for change within the sponsoring organization.

To extend beyond traditional approaches it should:

- Be aligned with key business objectives.
- Identify strategic gaps that must be closed to achieve the objectives.

- Assess more than environmental issues.
- Provide a thorough examination of internal and external changes that impact employee attitudes and behaviors.
- Include an assessment of systemic, management and leadership, and human factors.
- Provide clear benchmarks against which employees can measure diversity outcomes.

Rapidly-changing indicators should be tracked more frequently, while factors that tend to change more slowly can be examined at longer intervals. Since research shows that diversity work has significant impacts on major organizational objectives (e.g., voluntary attrition, stock price, profitability, enrollment or membership) in 18–24 months, measurements should be taken at least that often. Hiring, promotions, complaints, and more rapidly occurring human resource changes should be measured quarterly. If cost-effective technology is available, continuous measurement can also be worthwhile.

SIX AREAS FOR MEASUREMENT

Six key diversity areas for which measurements should be developed are: program evaluation, representation, workplace climate, benchmarks and best practices, external recognition, and relating diversity to overall performance. Each of these indicators is discussed below.

Program Evaluation

Every diversity activity or event (e.g., training sessions, mentoring, celebrations, resource groups, pay equity analyses) should be evaluated. At a minimum, such evaluations must ask three questions: What went well or what is working well? What could have gone better or needs improvement? What overall rating do observers give the activity or event?

This simple three-point evaluation is a firm starting point; however, better program evaluations go beyond the starting point. They link programmatic activities with outcomes such as performance changes noted by subordinates, peers, supervisors, customers, and clients; impacts on team or group productivity; and overall organizational performance in quality, enrollments, financial indicators, costs, cycle time, and the like. More sophisticated instruments can be used, of course, and activities with large numbers of participants may require more easily compiled numerical data.

Representation

The population of the organization should be studied with respect to the flow of people through it. Look at the flow in, up, and out of the organization, and analyze it with regard to demographic factors. Who is represented here?

At a minimum, this measure usually includes age, sex, race, and sometimes disability. Information on national origin, education, veteran status, marital status, and languages spoken may also be available and is often useful to examine. As trust levels rise and the climate for diversity improves, data on more sensitive differences will become accessible (e.g., mental disability, sexual orientation, family demographics, religious practices). Measuring more than race and sex reinforces an inclusive definition of diversity, essential to reducing resistance and preventing backlash against diversity change.

The goal of representation measurement is to guarantee equity and progress toward diversity goals in recruitment, training and professional development, promotion, and retention. This aim includes achieving diversity at every organizational level.

Workplace Climate

This area of measurement is intended to determine whether or not the quality of work life is equitable across groups and individuals. Differences across groups suggest the presence of personal or institutional biases and "-isms." Differences across individuals should be closely examined. They are somewhat more acceptable than group differences, as they are more likely to be a function of unique circumstances and more likely to change for the better as all human resource processes improve.

A wide range of tools can and should be used to measure climate. The most common tool is a survey comprised of fixed-response and open-ended questions. Surveys provide ease of analysis and statistical rigor. Without open-ended items they are limited with regard to qualitative matters.

Another common method of data gathering is the focus group. In this procedure small, homogeneous, and heterogeneous groups of 5–15 people are interviewed with a uniform set of questions. The results are recorded and analyzed for contents and themes. Data from focus groups can be used effectively to design a wider quantitative survey. The advantage of the focus group is its richness of input. Disadvantages are the lack of representative sampling and the uncertain statistical significance of the findings.

A third kind of workplace climate measurement might be described as indirect or unobtrusive measures. For qualitative data, these measures might be based on informal reports or observations made during a walkabout through the organization. Quantitatively, they might keep count of complaints (internal and external), litigation, and voluntary turnover. Differences across groups may reveal specific diversity needs.

Benchmarks and Best Practices

As organizations seek to determine how well they are doing and what they should be doing, benchmarking and best-practices studies—custom-designed and specific to the company—become excellent sources of information. There is a growing base of literature about best practices in diversity. Ann Morrison's *The New Leaders* (1992), for example, describes the full range of diversity practices used in major corporations. Morrison also provides some evaluative input regarding importance and perceived effectiveness. Most large consulting firms doing diversity work also have data on what the best companies are doing.

External Recognition

Many organizations have set a goal of being a preferred employer, university of choice, or best place to work. Receiving recognition as a "best" from an external source is one indication of status or progress. One can also analyze the criteria that are used by external sources and adopt them for internal evaluation.

These criteria will, at a minimum, help the organization answer the question, "How good do we have to be in order to be recognized by others?"

The number of such "best" resources continues to grow and includes an increasing diversity of criteria and targets. They include:

- Top companies for working mothers—*Good Housekeeping.*
- America's most admired corporations—*Fortune.*
- Best companies for women—*Business Week.*
- Best places for Hispanics to work—*Hispanic.*
- Top 10 places for gay and lesbian workers—*The Advocate.*
- *The Best Companies for Minorities* by Lawrence Otis Graham (Penguin Books, 1993).
- *The 100 Best Companies to Work for in America* by Robert Levering and Milton Moskowitz (Penguin Books, 1994).

Relating Diversity to Overall Performance

Effective diversity work leads to measurable improvements in overall organizational performance. Measurement systems should incorporate elements that examine the relationship between the specific diversity work being done and the key or desired organizational outcomes.

Recommended research and measurement questions in this area include:

- What impact can be observed on overall performance as we address a larger number of differences among employees and customers or clients?
- What specific additional issues—over and above race, gender, disabilities, cross-functional teaming, and age— have explicit impacts on the performance of our organization?
- What intra-organization, intra-industry, and intra-sector refinements should be made to diversity measurement technology?

SUMMARY

- Effective diversity initiatives identify business objectives, identify development gaps, specify accountabilities, and monitor progress regularly through periodic measurement and evaluation.
- Measurement is critical because tangible evidence gets noticed, shows progress, can be supported in the budget, and is vital to ongoing refinement and adjustment.
- Every diversity event or action should be evaluated, linking the activity as closely as possible to key desired organizational outcomes.
- Representation within the organization must be assessed throughout the pipeline, from pre-hire recruitment through involuntary turnover.
- The workplace climate for individuals and groups must be examined in terms of perceptions and behavior. Do differences in climate correlate with diversity issues?
- Success in diversity is supported by benchmarking with other organizations to identify best practices.
- Recognition by external sources is one indicator of excellence. These sources name best places to work in general and best places for members of specific groups.
- Good macro indicators of success with diversity are overall organizational performance and status as a preferred provider of goods and services.

8

CHAPTER

Conducting a Successful Diversity Audit

A diversity audit provides up-to-date and useful information about diversity-related issues in the organization. In addition, audit information plays a valuable role in shaping or redefining a diversity initiative. Data collected as part of the audit can also identify supports and constraints surrounding existing or proposed diversity processes.

In this chapter we will discuss each of the steps leading to the completion of a successful diversity audit. At the conclusion of the chapter, we will provide a list of the key management roles that will help make the diversity audit successful.

IDENTIFY THE RATIONALE

Organizations conduct diversity audits at different times and for different reasons. If the institution first identifies clear and specific audit objectives, the audit is more likely to yield the desired results. Here are three common and valid reasons for implementing a diversity audit:

1. Organizations that already have some experience with diversity frequently conduct an audit at the urging of a single

division or department. Desire for an audit may be strong, for example, in a corporate division well along in its diversity effort. By an audit, the division seeks a way to measure progress and assess the effectiveness of its work to date.

2. Other organizations or parts of organizations call for an audit before beginning a diversity initiative. Audit information is invaluable when it is used in conjunction with an initial needs assessment. It helps the organization to clearly identify its diversity issues, assess its organizational needs, develop appropriate interventions, and establish a baseline from which to measure future progress.

3. A third strong reason for diversity audits is to identify diversity issues impacting a specific sector or function within the organization. For example, litigation may indicate that the company has a problem recruiting and retaining people of color and women for particular departments. Or the company may be concerned that diversity is not reflected in product development and marketing. Managers, for example, may wish to identify diversity-related issues in units responsible for the development and promotion of products and services aimed at diverse buyers or specific market niches, such as Hispanics or people with disabilities.

SECURE SENIOR MANAGEMENT SUPPORT

Without visible support by senior management, a major organizational initiative such as diversity quickly can lose momentum. Active support of the team managing a division or department is especially important when implementing a diversity audit.

Individuals initiating or leading the audit should keep four rules in mind as they seek support of the management team:

1. Provide a clear, concise, and easy-to-understand rationale for the audit. A strong rationale is especially important when senior management did not specifically initiate the audit.
2. Keep the management team informed of current and ongoing audit-related activities.
3. Keep the information simple.
4. Clearly communicate management's role in implementing a successful audit.

If senior managers specifically requested the diversity audit, their input and involvement should be solicited actively at each step. Management team members should have the opportunity to direct the process and advise on procedures. They may also wish to review survey questions before they are finalized and review materials announcing the audit. These are management team concerns, because management must respond to every area of audit results, especially in areas where action is not forthcoming.

CONDUCT INTERVIEWS AND FOCUS GROUPS

As we said in Chapter 7, it is important to conduct one-on-one interviews and focus groups before the audit in order to uncover the main diversity-related issues and identify major survey categories. Survey questions based on focus group and interview responses will be on target and more likely to gather useful, relevant information. A preliminary survey document can be developed from just a few interviews and focus groups, then customized and expanded as subsequent responses become available.

All members of senior management should be interviewed one-on-one. Then, depending on the factors driving the audit, groups and individuals from different categories of employees— women, people of color, individuals in unique work roles (e.g., summer interns), older workers, younger workers, new employees, long-time employees, etc.—should be interviewed.

Focus groups familiarize diversity professionals with the varying perspectives of different groups within the organization. The process allows each group to share its specific issues and describe the company's diversity environment from its special point of view. Input from focus groups also gives the diversity professional a better understanding of differences and similarities in the perspectives of the several categories. Such understanding is exceptionally helpful in developing and refining a survey instrument to focus on relevant issues and concerns.

PREPARE A DETAILED COMMUNICATION STRATEGY

Communication strategy for the audit must include clear pre-audit communication, clear communication of the results, and clear follow-up actions.

Pre-Audit Announcement

Communication starts with an announcement about the intention to conduct a diversity audit. An effective announcement describes the time frame for the audit, how it will be conducted, who will be involved, and the importance of the effort. The announcement sets the tone for the entire audit process and follow-up actions. It must be positive and enthusiastic, and strongly emphasize management support. An effective announcement also describes the rationale for the audit, how information will be shared with employees, and what will happen after the audit.

Audit Results

Individuals responding to any type of climate survey share a common concern: "Will something be done or is this a waste of time? Is this another case where they ask for my input but never follow up?" People responding to an audit survey need to be assured that the findings will be shared and that they will be told in advance what will be done with the findings.

Follow-Up Actions

Even in pre-audit announcements it is important to be as specific as possible about how the organization will follow up on high-priority items. Employees might be told, for example, that sub-committees or task forces will be formed to address specific issues disclosed by the audit and to plan the next steps.

The organization should, of course, begin work on specific issues as quickly as possible after the audit. It is more effective to begin work and communicate progress frequently (however limited) than to postpone reporting until a major milestone has been reached. Work in progress can be communicated via newsletters, bulletin boards, department meetings, or by a combination of these vehicles.

Planning and communicating follow-up actions also provides an excellent opportunity to gain employee involvement in the diversity process itself. Employees should be able to choose ways they find comfortable from a range of activities—from conducting additional interviews or research, to joining a newly formed committee, to serving as liaison to a different department in the company.

CREATE AUDIT CATEGORIES

Some major organizational categories influenced by diversity are organizational culture and environment, leadership and management practices, systems, supervisory practices, and human factors. Categories such as these make a good starting point for survey development. Information gathered through interviews and focus groups can then be used to refine the outline with additional categories or subheadings.

It is important to remember during survey development what factors within each category need to be measured and what information is needed to draw sound conclusions. Take organizational culture and environment as an example. Perhaps several participants in the initial focus groups say the climate in the company is not supportive and accepting of diversity. This suggests a need for audit questions that specifically discover how many employees feel that way, how strongly, and what factors at work create or continue to support that perception.

Another criterion for useful audits is the degree to which the audit effort is tied to specific business objectives. For example, suppose an organization that is expanding globally wants to know if its internal systems and leadership practices need modification to respond appropriately to the global marketplace. In each survey category of the diversity audit, this organization would include questions designed to identify specific areas for improvement.

Ultimately the audit must help measure two factors: what *is* and what *should be*. With this information, gap analysis can identify what needs to be done to close the distance in each category between "is" and "should be." Well-designed survey instruments greatly facilitate gap analysis.

Finally, every survey should include a limited number of open-ended questions to invite employees' thoughts on high-priority issues or to identify additional concerns.

CONDUCT THE AUDIT

An audit survey can be administered on-site or mailed to employees' homes. The authors' research shows that most organizations get better participation on-site than through the mail.

The people and procedures in survey administration are also crucial to its overall success. A trust gap exists in many organizations, and where this is the case it is better to select an outside consultant to administer the survey and analyze the results.

If the surveys are not distributed and collected in a group setting, then mailboxes bearing the consultant's name and address should be clearly visible at each of the organization's locations. This allows employees to complete the surveys at their leisure and drop them in the boxes for transmittal to the consultant. To increase participation, secure a higher return rate, and reduce the fear that internal personnel may examine surveys, some organizations provide postage-paid envelopes imprinted with the consultant's address.

Space and time considerations also impact survey administration. Depending on the number of locations, physical facilities, and size of the survey group, some organizations set aside a portion of the cafeteria for several days and schedule group sessions to facilitate timely survey completion. Usually employees are offered their choice of several half-hour or 45-minute time slots. Other organizations schedule smaller sessions in available conference or meeting rooms, although this approach requires additional personnel to staff multiple locations.

Successful survey administration depends on how well the effort is planned and coordinated. Organizations working in close partnership with an outside consultant during planning and administration usually enjoy the smoothest audits.

ANALYZE RESULTS

A successful diversity audit encompasses both quantitative and qualitative analyses, coupled with gap identification. Gap identification indicates how frequently a particular factor occurs compared to how frequently it ought to occur—the *is* and the *should be* we discussed earlier in the chapter.

The final audit report should prioritize the results and information presented by concluding with short-term, tactical actions as well as broader, more long-term recommendations.

COMMUNICATE RESULTS

Shortly after the audit survey, all employees should get a "thanks for your participation" memo. Several follow-up communications should keep people updated while the final report is being prepared. At the time the report is issued, management should issue a statement indicating that it is reviewing the data and that further information will be forthcoming.

Other methods of communicating results include newsletters and debriefing sessions. At Bayer Agricultural Division, department managers were debriefed on the results and trained to deliver the information to employees in their respective departments. Senior managers of each department introduced the session and showed their support of the process before handing the presentation over to department managers.

DEVELOP ACTION PLANS

If the diversity audit is conducted throughout the organization, it is best to create a supplemental report for each business unit. This approach allows departments and divisions to begin work quickly on the issues of greatest significance to them. It also allows each business unit to link the diversity effort to its specific business objectives and performance criteria.

When the audit is conducted within an individual business unit, it is best to ask representatives of the unit to help clarify and prioritize key issues. At General Mills Information Systems, for example, the organization conducted a survey debriefing and planning session. The session brought diverse focus groups (the same people involved in the creation of the survey) in to rank and define diversity issues that were most important to them. While sharing their perspectives, needs, and expectations, each group also made recommendations that the organization could use in dealing with the key audit findings. Compiling the data made it easier to determine priority issues as a whole and to develop tactical action plans.

Another issue in developing an audit action plan is the need to set the stage and create enthusiasm. Bayer Agricultural Division provides an excellent example. The diversity council started by getting senior management involved with input and support from day one.

Clear messages from senior management sparked that commitment. Hermann Werner, president of Bayer Agriculture, and Helge Wehmeier, CEO of Bayer USA, let it be known that commitment to diversity and support for culture change was at the top of Bayer's agenda. Both continued to show their support through daily involvement and frequent reinforcement. They monitored the progress of the initiative and periodically followed up with those involved.

The diversity council also worked for buy-in and commitment by every employee. To ensure that employees would be willing to respond to the audit survey, the council asked for worker input regarding survey administration. Employees could choose whether to answer the survey in-house or have it mailed to their homes.

Once the survey was distributed, a series of communications helped build excitement and generate commitment to its completion. "Reminder" buttons, which in this case were computer generated stick ons with reminders, such as 'Have you mailed in your survey?' or TWO DAYS LEFT! and so on, were sent every day for a week before the end of the survey period. As further reinforcement, members of the council visited each department to ask employees to return their surveys. Additional reminders went by e-mail and loudspeaker. The media blitz resulted in a 60 percent return. By comparison, many internal surveys achieve return rates far below 50 percent.

MANAGEMENT ROLES IN A SUCCESSFUL DIVERSITY AUDIT

As we have said numerous times, management's commitment to the diversity process is critical at this juncture; it sets the stage for all future diversity work. There are four key management roles that will help make the diversity audit successful: leader, motivator, communicator, and learner. Each of these roles requires specific actions, as outlined below:

Leader
- Identify and examine your own biases and attitudes about diversity and the audit in particular.
- Have a clear contextual understanding of the organization's diversity goal and process, especially regarding how it links to business strategy and objectives.

- Make sure you understand the goal and objectives of the diversity audit. Make sure you understand the process to carry out the audit. Communicate that process to employees.
- Listen and observe. Be sensitive. Stay attuned to employees' reactions and expectations regarding the diversity audit.
- Create a safe environment for the audit by supporting and encouraging open, honest dialogue about it.

Motivator

- Share a strong sense of urgency about the audit.
- Take every opportunity to promote the audit.
- Build anticipation.
- Encourage involvement by participating fully in the process.

Communicator

- Be candid and truthful about the reasons for the audit.
- Be constructive. Guard against counterproductive comments about the audit or the diversity process in general.
- Be consistent. Communicate the same message with the same enthusiasm to your employees as you do to your own manager.

Learner

- When the audit is finished, be open to the data and the diverse perspectives of the respondents.
- Continue to work on your personal diversity journey.

SUMMARY

- A diversity audit plays a valuable role in shaping or redefining a diversity initiative.
- Begin the audit by identifying the rationale for it.

- Generate commitment and support by getting management involved from the start. Audits can help secure senior management support for diversity work, as well.
- Interviews and focus groups can be a part of the audit process as well as be used to help design surveys.
- A communication strategy must include pre-audit communication, communication of the results, and clear follow-up actions.
- Major audit categories include organizational culture and environment, leadership and management practices, supervisory behavior, systems and procedures, and human factors.
- Gather and analyze qualitative and quantitative data.
- The people and procedures in survey administration, as well as space and time considerations, are important factors.
- Focus on gap analysis—what *is* compared to what *should be*.
- Localize the planning of post-audit actions.
- It is important to set the stage and create enthusiasm about the audit.
- Management plays four key roles that will help make the diversity audit successful: leader, motivator, communicator, and learner.

9

CHAPTER

The Diversity Change Process, Step by Step

This chapter on the diversity change process is for readers interested in a step-by-step overview that focuses on actions to consider as an organization progresses through the process. It is oriented toward readers who are not diversity professionals and may therefore be less interested in research-based developmental models. Instead, we provide an overview model for success which outlines a five-phase diversity initiative. We will also offer brief vignettes to illustrate specific aspects of the process.

The five phases of the diversity change process are as follows: (1) creating awareness of diversity change; (2) transition; (3) accepting change; (4) institutionalization; and (5) aligning diversity with organizational goals and values.

CREATING AWARENESS

Many organizations that undertake diversity initiatives experience some form of diversity backlash. White males are a common source of backlash. Another is internal or external stakeholders in the company who do not believe that a particular group (e.g., gays and lesbians) should be part of the diversity definition. A third source is long-oppressed groups that feel newly powerful in organizations under pressure from boycotts or litigation. Such groups are apt to expect instant change, and when diversity efforts don't produce it, they lash out too.

Backlash can be minimized or avoided by thorough preparation. Here are five precautionary steps to build into the preparation of a diversity initiative:

1. Guide the organization's original change agents through the learning process. Actively involve them in defining diversity, aligning it with the vision of the organization, setting a direction, and in beginning their personal diversity work.

2. Share results of the diversity needs assessment with all employees and communicate specific actions that may or will be taken as a result of the findings.

3. Establish organizational forums in which employees can ask questions, share their concerns, and discuss the change process without fear of reprisal.

4. Keep members abreast of the process and remind them frequently of their stake in it.

5. Communicate the message of diversity in a positive, nonthreatening, respectful manner. The organization's ability to make members feel that they are part of the process from the very beginning is the key to a successful introduction.

An Example of Creating Awareness

An international company in the energy industry launched a diversity initiative in the early 1990s. The company provided people, funding, and substantial support for the launch. Small groups of internal professionals teamed up with selected consultants to design the initiative. The effort included needs assessments and well-designed training. Senior executives participated in early training sessions. Many other elements required for success were also present.

However, with few exceptions, involvement in design and initial implementation was limited to selected individuals and groups. While news of the initiative appeared in company newsletters, for most employees involvement was defined as participating in training events. It took the company three to four years to move beyond early phases of the work.

In those years the company was hampered by a lack of employee involvement and the absence of linkages between diversity and other major initiatives, such as restructuring and reengineering. As these flaws in the design were addressed, participation broadened and linkages to other change efforts were created. Momentum increased. By 1996 the company was poised to leverage a large base of employee support through councils, task forces, training, extensive employee communication, and opinion-sharing processes.

TRANSITION

During the transition phase organizations begin to integrate diversity awareness into their day-to-day operations. Integration is achieved when an organization's members live by diversity values. While many organizations include diversity in statements describing their values, most employees find it difficult to translate these statements into actual behaviors.

During transition the expectations of senior management may rise. Once managers and other change agents have clearly identified diversity issues (through assessment), they are motivated to "solve" those problems as soon as possible. For successful problem solving, managers must appreciate the foundations of a good transition phase.

Understanding the Change

Once the organization has completed a diversity needs assessment, it must share the findings with all employees. It also must prioritize the issues and communicate those priorities so employees understand which issues will be dealt with first. There must be a visible long-term commitment to having a positive impact on every participant in the organization; everyone must anticipate some personal benefit. In addition, each major diversity activity must be supported by follow-up communication to ensure that employees are able to track the progress that the organization is making.

Sharing the data gathered during the assessment shows employees that diversity issues relate to everyone in the organization. It helps people understand what's in it for them and how the initiative will affect them personally.

Finally, because change is difficult for everyone, it is essential that the organization "overcommunicate" as a way to help all employees deal positively with the events happening around them.

Implementing the Diversity Initiative

Next, the organization must develop a cohesive strategy that ties together disparate efforts such as business planning, human resource planning, quality, education and training, networks, councils, and newsletters. These efforts should work interdependently, with high regard for the way they fit together to accomplish the organization's overall objectives.

Ingredients of such a comprehensive plan include:

- Analyzing assessment data and prioritizing needs to determine what actions will be taken first.
- Developing a communications strategy to inform employees of each activity, its overall objective, and how it relates to other efforts.
- Identifying specific linkages between each activity and the institution's overall objectives.
- Identifying a measurement methodology and how it will be used to monitor progress of the entire initiative and of individual efforts within the initiative.

See Figure 9–1 for a visual description of an integrated diversity strategy.

The primary management responsibilities in the transition phase are strategic planning linked to organizational objectives, ongoing maintenance of each initiative, development of employee support, attention to feedback, and willingness to modify and adapt as needed.

FIGURE 9-1

Diversity: An Integrated Approach

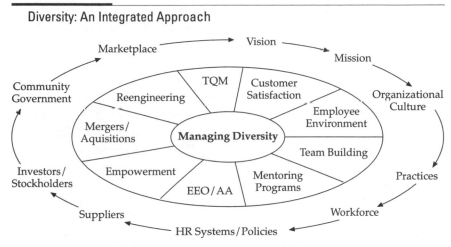

ADAPTATION: SHAPING THE DIVERSITY INITIATIVE

The success of any initiative depends on how well it is managed. Some organizations hope that the mere delivery of diversity training will solve their problems and generate benefits from diversity. But ongoing monitoring and management of each initiative is essential to help shape and move the process forward. Careful attention to internal and external changes is also necessary, so that strategies can be modified when necessary.

In one organization, for example, it became apparent that awareness training had already accomplished its primary objective: employees were aware of diversity as an organizational goal, could define the concept, and could state the rationale for the process.

To move forward, the organization needed to link future training to the achievement of specific objectives. The consumer marketing department recognized that its customer base was becoming more diverse, while the staff serving that base was homogeneous and lacked life experience with racial diversity. When they dealt with the company, customers saw no racial or gender diversity in the staff. In addition to not projecting a diverse image, the staff also did not have the awareness and skills it needed to be effective in the new market.

A training program to address these deficits included activities designed to help employees understand the cultural norms, traditions, and behaviors of their customers. The training introduced specific skills to help employees interact more effectively with these customers. The training was followed by periodic audits of participants' interactions with their customers. A new customer satisfaction survey included questions asking new customers how well the company understood and met their needs.

The transition phase in diversity change is a golden opportunity to reassess and regain control of diversity efforts. It is the time to find out what is working, what is not working, and how future efforts must be shaped to respond to unanticipated factors. Organizations have to ask, "Are we getting the desired outcomes from implementation of this initiative?" If not, it is time to reshape or rethink the process.

ACCEPTING CHANGE

Following planning and implementation of a diversity initiative, organizations must continue their efforts to secure employee and management commitment. The first step in securing commitment is fostering a realization that diversity is not a "flavor of the month" program. Rather, it will be integrated in overall operations and will not go away. Organizations demonstrate their commitment and sincerity through ongoing investment in the resources necessary to create lasting cultural change.

Real commitment goes beyond the organization's initial intention to engage in a diversity process. Many organizations launch diversity initiatives believing that strong commitment already exists; in reality, a thorough understanding of the depth and breadth of the undertaking must be sought continuously.

Many companies assume that diversity is a finite program and that sponsoring a few diversity workshops will solve sticky issues of difference among employees. In reality, true acceptance of diversity change occurs when the organization positions diversity as a process, not as a program. Individual acceptance begins when employees recognize the comprehensive nature of the process and view it as an ongoing fact of life rather than as an isolated event.

Developing this awareness, however, does not mean that employees are necessarily happy about the change or willing to participate. A person may feel threatened by diversity, for example, but still agree to learn about it and gain new skills (i.e., learn new behaviors without changing attitudes) in order to be successful in the organization. Likewise, an autocratic CEO may continue to be autocratic, but start allowing others on the management team to voice their opinions without fear of retaliation.

Several factors differentiate ongoing commitment from the initial good intentions that launch most diversity efforts. Ongoing commitment is present when employees at all levels:

- Understand what diversity means to them personally and to the organization as a whole.
- Become involved in the process for their own personal reasons.
- Continue actively exploring diversity and its implications.
- Sincerely believe that the organization is in it for the long haul.
- Begin to modify their behavior relative to diversity.

This level of individual commitment by employees must be encouraged and matched by their company's institutional commitment. For its own integrity and to sustain momentum, the organization will strive to ensure that:

- Employees understand the meaning of diversity and acknowledge a wide range of reasons to focus on it.
- Vehicles are in place to help employees deal with their personal concerns regarding the process and its impact on them.
- Employees are kept informed of diversity activities and diversity interventions throughout the organization.
- There is a structure for and a constant focus on process renewal.
- Tools to measure diversity change are in place and used throughout the organization.
- Initial assessment data are used as a baseline from which to measure progress.

INSTITUTIONALIZING CHANGE

At this stage the diversity process has stimulated significant changes in the organization and has affected the company culture. From the external environment to internal operations, diversity is alive, well, and thriving. Stakeholders can see visible changes throughout the organization, including these typical signs of an altered culture:

- More people throughout the organization are invested in the diversity process.
- Reactions to diversity are more positive and enthusiastic.
- Organizational systems are open to changes that make them more supportive of a diverse workforce and a diverse customer or client base.
- Measurement of diversity progress is continuous.
- There is a renewed focus on the people side of the enterprise and on internal and external customer relations.
- Members of the institution are responsible and accountable for diversity change on personal and organizational levels; they no longer view it as the sole responsibility of the human resources or personnel department.
- Ongoing diversity education supports the goals of the enterprise.

Here are some more specific signs of diversity change at a healthily institutionalized stage:

- Diversity sessions are led primarily by internal people from all levels and units. They do this along with their regular roles or duties.
- Diversity celebrations (e.g., Chinese American Week, U.N. Children's Day, Grandparents' Day, Veterans' Day, Cinco de Mayo, Festival of the First Fruits, National Coming Out Day, Susan B. Anthony Day, Fathers' Day, International Working Women's Day, Kwanzaa) are themselves diverse, creative, and educational, and are enjoyed throughout the organization.
- Team organizers automatically think about many types of diversity as they select team members. Employees consider homogeneous teams boring.

- Diversity progress is reported along with functional, enrollment, service delivery, and financial results.
- People involved with the company—internally and outside—feel valued and will say so.
- The fiscal and human resources that support specific diversity programs come from their natural organizational locations, not always from a human resources or diversity department. Diverse team-building, for example, comes from the group that assists team building. Diversity in product marketing is generated by the marketing people. Strategies for selling across cultures come from sales.
- Diversity education and training are ongoing; they are internally designed and delivered, part of the standard training curriculum, and part of every training course.

ALIGNING DIVERSITY WITH COMPANY GOALS AND VALUES

This is the stage that diversity efforts aim for. Effective initiatives include the objective of integrating diversity with other processes and binding them all together through the mission, vision, and values of the organization. An organization has reached this stage when:

- Most of an organization's employees exhibit values-driven behavior day to day.
- The organization's management practices, environment, leadership, and structure continuously support values-driven behavior.
- A vehicle exists to test and adjust the alignment of individual and organizational strategies and to identify or reduce obstacles to alignment.
- The diversity process is disciplined yet flexible, and capable of mid-course corrections.
- The organization facilitates open, honest, and ongoing communication, ranging from the big picture to the tactical issues that impact the organization and its employees.

SUMMARY

- The diversity change process is comprised of five phases: (1) creating awareness; (2) transition; (3) accepting change; (4) institutionalization; and (5) aligning diversity with company goals and values.
- Creating awareness requires dealing with backlash, primarily through participation, inclusiveness, and two-way communication.
- Transition is facilitated by helping everyone understand and track the change, strategic planning, a comprehensive initiative, and continuous shaping to fit the needs and culture of the organization.
- Acceptance or adoption of diversity change involves maintaining the commitment, personal diversity work, and ongoing assessment and feedback.
- Institutionalization is evident when large numbers of people are involved in diversity work, individual reactions are generally positive, all systems reflect diversity, and there is ongoing education, training, and measurement.
- Alignment is achieved when day-to-day behavior is values-driven, leaders and managers model appropriate behavior, and diversity is monitored as an integral feature of individual and organizational strategies.

10

CHAPTER

Revitalizing Traditional Diversity Initiatives

Many organizations have already been doing diversity work for several years. Some of them are getting mixed results, seeing them as too costly to continue, not making progress as fast as they desire, or simply running out of steam. How can such organizations revitalize their diversity initiatives and move ahead? This chapter describes several ways to address this situation. It deals with training, ongoing justification, networks, organizational systems, and management practices.

AWARENESS TRAINING

Thousands of organizations have already sponsored some form of diversity awareness training for employees. This type of training is effective in increasing employees' basic understanding of diversity. By itself, however, awareness training does not adequately establish the comprehensive conceptual framework necessary for effective, ongoing diversity processes.

Most awareness training, for example, still focuses on issues of race and gender. This limitation sometimes creates a destructive "us versus them" dichotomy among participants, which may keep some employees from accepting and actively contributing to the diversity process. Many trainers report that participant reactions to introductory diversity sessions are more negative when the sessions focus specifically on race or gender. By contrast, reactions to general diversity introductions and sessions on style or cross-functional team-building seem more positive.

A commonly observed reaction since the 1980s—even to race and gender training under a diversity umbrella—has been "This diversity stuff is just affirmative action with a new name." For those who had positive experiences with affirmative action, this usually is not a problem. But poorly implemented affirmative action often plants negative seeds, so that anything which even hints at it now causes discomfort. Therefore, effective contemporary training must distinguish appropriate from inappropriate affirmative action and position diversity effectively.

Effective positioning means that diversity is defined inclusively and that affirmative action is equitably applied whenever underrepresentation needs to be addressed proactively. Of course the relevant categories include race and gender, but they go substantially beyond them, as well.

Women, people of color, and all advocates for race and gender issues must be convinced that diversity efforts will address their concerns in depth. People concerned about race and gender must also hear that a more inclusive introduction is essential before in-depth examination begins. Individuals who need to address race and gender, but are not motivated to do so, must be convinced that their issues will be addressed, too.

Thus, the inclusive definition of diversity implies an explicit contract by which everyone agrees that a broad range of issues will be addressed individually and in depth. Self-interest can be acknowledged in a bargain that says, "I'll give my full attention to what matters to you, if you'll do the same for me." Such an agreement is especially important to those in early personal developmental stages with respect to diversity issues.

Effective diversity work starts wherever you are, and goes forward from there.

In addition to an early and inclusive definition of diversity, training also must address the question of *why* diversity matters. This question should be examined in terms of personal and organizational benefits such as communication skills, negotiation abilities, client demographics, marketing, sales, recruitment, and retention. Once compelling justifications with explicit benefits are identified, an ongoing stream of reminders must be provided.

A tool company provides a good example. The company operates in an historically traditional and male-dominated industry. While the benefits of diversity make sense from an organizational perspective, many employees cannot personally relate to the full range of diversity issues, since they are part of the historic majority in their industry. Diversity training in this company started with a discussion about the many ways this seemingly homogeneous group actually differed within itself (e.g., age, style, function, level). These differences were then wrapped in a diversity package.

Building a compelling justification based on recognized ways in which current employees and customers differ is a good beginning for diversity work. From that point, new and less familiar or less comfortable differences can be added to the mix. Creating a climate in which differences in style, age, function, and level are recognized and accepted is beneficial for addressing race and gender later. In turn, addressing race and gender helps create a climate in which even more difficult issues, such as sexual orientation, can be explored.

In general, the more issues an organization explores, the more potential contributions to organizational goals and objectives are added. Each new issue can add discrete value and, in combination with other issues, create exponentially increasing value.

In the case of the tool company, only employees who worked primarily in sales had any contact with diverse customers. For most employees, life was good the way it was and there was little apparent reason to change the status quo. By doing a thorough assessment, however, the organization was able to frame the concept of diversity around issues that were relevant to the majority of the employees.

The assessment data revealed a perception that "no one retires from this organization." A significant number of employees believed that they needed to look for another job in their early 40s, because the company would not keep them after they reached 50. As a result, many top-performing employees (mostly white males) left the organization just as they reached their maximum potential. The unwritten rule ("you're out by 50") had an adverse effect on sales, too: When the company needed veteran sales representatives, there were none.

For this tool company, age became the "hook" by which the majority of employees became engaged in and committed to diversity and its benefits. Individuals could see clearly how addressing the overall issue would benefit them personally—they would no longer need to reestablish themselves in new organizations just because they were approaching middle age.

In similar cases, finding one or several diversity "hooks" often is essential to the successful launch or revitalization of a diversity initiative. The larger the number of employees committed to diversity work, the faster and easier the change process becomes. Starting with an issue of explicit self-interest helps build a foundation from which to address other issues where self-interest might not be as clearly evident. Such sequencing is also beneficial when an organization starts with issues that are comfortable and non-threatening for participants. What is learned from topics where comfort is high can be applied to more challenging issues. Skills should be built and supports should be developed before more difficult challenges are presented.

Personal relevance and real-life applications make it easier to involve the majority of employees in the diversity process. As mentioned earlier, these applications move people from the conceptual or "head" approach through the behavioral "hand" approach to the internalized or "heart" work that endures.

DIVERSITY NETWORKS AND COUNCILS

A popular diversity effort supported by many companies has been the creation of diversity networks and councils. In addition to accepting the traditional responsibility of providing support to diverse groups, networks (sometimes known as affinity or resource groups) can assist the organization in meeting its overall objectives. Progressive companies maximize the value of their diversity networks by using them as sounding boards or test groups for marketing and sales strategies.

For example, Avon's success in the American ethnic or multicultural markets is credited to the company's proactive multicultural hiring, upward mobility, and retention efforts. These efforts proved especially effective in sales and marketing.

The Pillsbury Company also provides examples of new market entries facilitated by the participation of multicultural professionals. These professionals brought their ethnic and culturally diverse backgrounds to the table in support of overall corporate objectives. This occurred most visibly in new product development, customization of existing products, marketing to new customers, and sales in new markets.

Pillsbury's successes occurred in both international and domestic markets. Spanish-speaking employees helped with language issues as business expanded into Spanish-speaking markets. Other ethnic networks provided new product ideas. For instance, a gay and lesbian resource group pointed out that annual household income in their community was approximately $20,000 higher than the national average, making the gay and lesbian market an ideal focus for upscale products.

Some diversity networks extend their efforts beyond simply making suggestions to the organization. They actively engage in community outreach and other programs to help the organization enhance its image and achieve its organizational objectives. The Pillsbury Black Network carried out a successful campaign to raise funds for the United Negro College Fund. As a result, the group and Pillsbury were recognized by the Fund for their high achievement. The company's image was undoubtedly enhanced within the African-American community—and possibly beyond.

Indeed, Pillsbury has received numerous unsolicited citations for excellence in diversity for its strong support of employee resource groups, community philanthropy, enhanced quality of work life, and improved performance in the multicultural marketplace. These citations include recognition from the Governor of Minnesota, articles in *The Wall Street Journal, Essence* magazine, and coverage by newspapers and television stations in locations in which it has plants and headquarters. The company's eight employee resource groups deserve much of the credit for this recognition.

Other examples of the successful work of diversity networks abound. An Asian employee network in one organization helped the company create business partnerships with an institution in China, opening the way for further relationship development. As part of the process, network members met with key company players responsible for developing the relationship with the company in China. The network members coached the corporate representatives on culture, norms, traditions, values, and business behaviors considered proper and appropriate in China.

In addition, some Asian network members traveled to China along with the executives, as part of the team charged to negotiate the partnership. The outcome has been a positive and successful business relationship between the two companies. The value the organization places on the Asian network has also grown, and the network is viewed as a critical link between the two companies.

Similar stories appeared in the media late in 1995, when General Motors (GM) signed a production-venture agreement with Shanghai Automotive Industry Corporation, China's largest automobile manufacturer. GM's success was directly attributed to the work of employees who understood the language and cultural requirements for doing business in China. These GM employees had or developed personal relationships that significantly supported a business venture. Both GM and the employees who led the effort gave credit to intercultural knowledge and relationships for the company's success in China's market.

Other organizations with employee resource groups that contribute explicitly to overall organization success include DuPont, U.S. West, Honeywell, and Ford.

KEY ORGANIZATIONAL SYSTEMS

An area that seems to be neglected consistently by diversity work is key organizational systems such as recruitment, hiring, retention, performance management, and succession planning. While these systems are actually the fuel that runs the corporate engine, most diversity efforts place their focus on training interventions instead. Yet, after 30 days most people retain only 10 percent of the content of a training workshop or seminar. If real behavior change is to take place, an organization needs more than training; it needs to create an environment and systems that support and encourage appropriate and effective behaviors.

A thorough and effective needs assessment provides important information about employee perceptions of their working environment and the extent to which organizational systems support or interfere with development of an inclusive environment.

The following are key tenets and characteristics of organizational systems that support diversity:

- They are aligned with and respond to changes in the workforce. Flexible work life and elder care policies, for example, recognize the demands placed on aging employees who may have to care for their own growing children and for aging parents at the same time.

- They are carefully planned. Beginning with an assessment of existing systems, policies are continuously monitored with an eye toward improvements to ensure that they produce the required results. The objective of maintaining alignment between employee needs and current and future systems is always uppermost in planners' minds.

- They have been shaped through the input of those affected.

- They include specific monitoring and measurement mechanisms to identify specific performance gaps and changes needed for better outcomes.

MANAGEMENT AND LEADERSHIP PRACTICES

The cliché "walking your talk" is, perhaps, the most difficult diversity work, particularly for managers and leaders. Yet diversity work is really about implementation and execution—to coin another phrase, you really must "just do it!" Organizations looking to reenergize existing initiatives may want to reexamine their values. Are leaders, managers, and the entire organization actually living by their stated values?

Self-evaluation and exploration also enhance diversity management and leadership. Improvement grows from personal learning and experience. It requires moving beyond one's personal comfort zone. People are not "taught" diversity; they discover it through personal experience.

Diversity management and leadership practices include:

- Believing in the values of the organization.
- Modeling behavior that embodies the organization's values.
- Creating an environment in which all people feel valued and respected.
- Engaging in self-exploration and self-assessment of one's own attitudes and feelings about diversity.
- Creating personal opportunities to gain experience and build relationships with others who are different from oneself.
- Being held accountable or holding oneself accountable for inappropriate behavior.
- Being willing to learn from experiences that focus on responsibility and risk, that move beyond one's comfort zones.

Organizations looking to revitalize their diversity initiatives should examine their performance in each of the areas described above. Such self-assessment is a large first step in identifying strategies to move the process forward.

A CHECKLIST FOR CONTINUOUS IMPROVEMENT

Organizational change and diversity management require constant attention and revitalization. Organizations should focus on continuous examination and improvement of their efforts, paying particular attention to the following:

- Nurture open, honest, and *ongoing* dialogue about diversity issues. Racism, sexism, and other "-isms" foster damaging divisions in organizations, communities, and society at large.
- Put mechanisms in place that encourage groups to continually assess their diversity-related strengths and areas for growth. Education and training should reinforce the achievement of diversity goals.
- Sustain an ongoing developmental focus on structures, systems, and practices that recognize, respect, support, and use diversity.

- Document and publicize success stories that tie diversity to improved individual, team, and organizational performance.
- Emphasize full integration of initiatives, such as diversity, quality, empowerment, reengineering, and restructuring. Although they may appear different, these initiatives have many similarities and often share common goals. Focus is diluted and resources are wasted when these efforts are sponsored as stand-alone programs. Tying all organizational efforts to a common vision and goal enhances the impact of communication and increases the likelihood of shared success.
- Work to minimize or eliminate gaps in trust, and to build effective communication between various groups in the organization.
- Learn from positive and negative experiences of others. Make the effort to use their knowledge to develop skills for successful personal and professional interactions.
- Assess and examine all areas of conflict in the organization. Misunderstandings may be the result of differences in style, language, culture, or other differences.

SUMMARY

- Many organizations' diversity initiatives falter after a few years.
- One frequently used first step in revitalizing an initiative is to expand education and training beyond race and gender while emphasizing inclusiveness.
- To lead organizations and individuals forward, begin where they are and go ahead from there.
- Reinforce the business case for diversity by using internal examples of failures and successes.
- Engaging in "heart" (emotional, affective) work can help move stalled individuals and organizations forward. This work helps participants "walk the talk" and behave consistently with stated values.

- Diversity networks councils can be created or renewed to facilitate progress.
- Employee resource groups or networks can also make explicit contributions to organizational performance and thereby add energy to diversity initiatives.

11
CHAPTER

Diversity Competencies

This final chapter outlines the key elements of diversity work, the major tasks to be performed, and the competencies required to conduct the tasks. The chapter concludes with a set of interview questions that may be useful for your own self-evaluation or for selecting individuals or teams to conduct diversity initiatives.

FIVE KEY ELEMENTS OF DIVERSITY WORK

Five key elements or concepts undergird successful diversity work. These are developmental stages, a balance between challenge and support, organizational and systems work, personal work, and diversity-general and diversity-specific work.

Developmental Stages

Diversity now has a knowledge base that is sufficient to describe the developmental stages through which individuals, groups, and organizations go as they become more effective in the context of diversity. Previous chapters have described several developmental models, behavior reflective of different phases of development, and actions designed to facilitate growth.

Effective diversity workers must recognize the need to sequence actions appropriately, the dangers of trying to skip stages, and the occasional necessity for recycling back to earlier stages. They also must know that people and organizations are at different stages on different issues and sometimes in different situations. Using this concept takes diversity work from a broad-brush, scattershot approach to one that is finely tuned and efficient.

A Balance Between Support and Challenge

To help individuals move forward through the phases of development, support and challenge must be strategically balanced. Diversity professionals typically begin with generous support for enhancing awareness and learning new, more effective behavioral skills. As skill levels rise, the level of challenge should rise as well, while the level of support declines. Eventually, new situations and opportunities will provide natural challenges. Moreover, success and the intrinsic satisfaction that accompanies it will provide support. Diversity leaders must continue to adjust the levels of challenge and support to maintain continuous improvement.

Organizational and Systems Work

Every organization has people-oriented and task-oriented systems that must be addressed in diversity work. Processes, practices, policies, and norms must be reviewed and modified to create a healthy and diverse environment. People processes and functional processes must both be addressed. Team forming and team-building systems must incorporate diversity—not only demographic diversity, but also diversity in style, function, and discipline.

Initially this systems work aims at removing barriers and eliminating inequities. Later, it focuses on creating a high-performance environment. Without systems work and systemic change, the benefits of diversity will not last.

Personal Work

While organizations must enhance their systems, individuals must also be enhanced. This happens through comprehensive personal work. Comprehensive work addresses both awareness and skills. It engages one mentally (new data, facts, and information), behaviorally (different words and deeds), and emotionally (healthier attitudes and feelings).

This is the familiar strong image of head, hand, and heart of which we have spoken throughout the book. Head and hand work help eliminate inappropriate and ineffective behaviors. They can and should be required of everyone in civilized organizations and societies. To achieve the highest level of health and effectiveness, heart work is needed as well. But because such work deals with personal feelings, it must not be coerced or mandated. Indeed, we believe that it is unethical to require heart work of anyone other than organizational and diversity leaders. Conducting heart work also requires a high skill level, described later in this chapter.

Diversity-General and Diversity-Specific Work

The most effective diversity initiatives begin by emphasizing that diversity is "*all* the ways in which we differ." They cover similarities as well as differences, while encouraging unity without uniformity.

Starting with diversity-general work builds a broad foundation and addresses everyone's fundamental responses to people who are different from them. A major theme is that diversity work must be done by all and will benefit all.

Failure to put this foundation in place before addressing specific issues is a major cause of resistance and backlash. Specific examples of diversity can and should be included in the early stages, but the emphasis should remain on inclusiveness. After the general base is in place, in-depth work can follow on particular issues. Both diversity-general and diversity-specific work are required for individuals and organizations to move past the middle stages of development.

SIX MAJOR TASKS

This section sketches the major tasks that are performed in successful diversity initiatives. They can be conveniently summarized under six headings: gaining commitment, conducting diagnoses, designing interventions, implementing the work, evaluating and exchanging feedback, and institutionalizing the work.

Gaining Commitment

The first task in a successful diversity initiative involves getting and sustaining support for the effort. Of primary importance is support from leaders who control resources, followed by the general support of all participants in the organization.

Diversity professionals articulate reasons for the work that are sufficiently compelling and inclusive to secure support from a wide range of individuals and groups. The rationales for diversity must resonate with people who have many—and often quite different—motivations. No single justification works for every individual, so arguments for diversity must be multifaceted. Intellectual and emotional arguments, empirical and anecdotal evidence all have their use in gaining commitment.

The case for diversity was presented in Chapter 1. Elements of an effective rationale include information on:

- Increasing individual effectiveness.
- Proactively dealing with social and demographic changes.
- Preventing and resolving litigation.
- Creating an environment of fairness and equity.
- Increasing productivity.
- Enhancing problem solving, creativity, and innovation.
- Contributing to the organization's growth and financial performance.

Once a compelling argument has been made, leaders also must be convinced that diversity work will be done professionally and cost effectively. Such competencies as research and communication skills are needed to build a strong case with a wide variety of employees. Integrity and honesty are critical as one begins to make promises about results to come for individuals and organizations.

Candor is crucial, too—acknowledging that internal complaints will rise as participants learn that the organization will hear them and address their needs. Persuasiveness is required to explain that both external and internal complaints ultimately will decline to record low levels. Optimism must be balanced with realism as one advocates diversity work. People of color and women who make the case for diversity must deal successfully with the challenge that it is their "visible" self-interest, not sound research, that leads them to see diversity as an asset.

Conducting Diagnoses

Before a diversity strategy can be developed, there must be accurate diagnoses at the individual, group, and organizational levels. Needs and issues must be identified. Phases of development (overall and issue-specific) must be discerned.

Many excellent diagnostic tools are available. A good starting point in the search for individual, group, and organizational assessment instruments is *Tools & Activities for a Diverse Work Force*, edited by Anthony Patrick Carnevale and S. Kanu Kogod (McGraw-Hill, 1996). For instruments to perform organizational assessments, refer to Marilyn Loden's *Implementing Diversity* (Irwin Professional Publishing, 1996). For additional individual assessment tools, see Sondra Thiederman's *Bridging Cultural Barriers for Corporate Success* and *Profiting in America's Multicultural Marketplace* (Lexington Books, 1991).

A specific individual-level assessment tool used in many organizations is *Discovering Diversity Profile* (Carlson Learning Co., 1994). This profile is designed to help individuals gain insight into their own knowledge, understanding, acceptance, and behavior regarding ways people differ. It deals very personally with age, race and ethnicity, gender, culture, disabilities, weight, job title, communication style, and status. Data from individuals can be aggregated for group or organization profiles, but only with extreme caution regarding privacy and confidentiality. Trust and safety must be paramount considerations in these areas of self-disclosure. The *Discovering Diversity Profile* instrument is consistent with Armida Mendez-Russell's model of individual development, discussed in Chapter 3.

The best diagnosticians use a variety of standardized, modified-standardized, and custom-designed instruments and methods. Methods range from informal observation to collection of perceptual data (surveys, focus groups) to sophisticated collection and analysis of quantitative data. Additional information on assessment can be found in Chapter 7, The Road to Results. These techniques are used to identify needs or issues, determine which problems and opportunities to address, and select appropriate interventions. Organizational assessment, organizational change, action research, and communication skills are central to the diagnosis task.

Designing Interventions

Designing appropriate interventions is the next key task. Successful interventions involve a great deal more than selecting and implementing the appropriate "10 best practices" found in the literature. Even a thorough comparative analysis of best practices or an in-depth benchmarking study will not yield appropriate guidance for a specific organization. Actions must be chosen and developmentally sequenced based on present reality and desired future states.

Actions must also fit the needs, opportunities, resources, culture, and style of the organization and individuals being addressed. Activities at individual, group, and organizational levels must fit together to complement each other and create synergies.

Education and training initiatives must begin with a compelling case for doing the work, an inclusive definition of diversity, and information on how the work will be conducted. Issue-specific work comes later.

Designing educational programs requires curriculum design and instructional systems skills. It also requires knowledge of learning styles and teaching techniques appropriate for the different styles.

Designing programs involving diversity engages substantive knowledge of the subject matter, skills to facilitate behavior change, and the ability to address emotional or affective content. Subject matter expertise must include diversity-general work and at least a few diversity-specific topics. Knowledge of how people and organizations grow and change is also critical for this task.

Work that addresses systems and processes must be done together with group and individual work. Both human resource systems (e.g., pre-recruitment, upward mobility, retention) and functional systems (e.g., product design, service delivery, education, research, sales, manufacturing, and administration) must be addressed.

Implementing the Work

Implementing diversity work is a complex task that, fortunately, has clear goals. The general goal is to enable everyone to create in others the feelings we associate with being among people like ourselves. Creating those feelings (e.g., camaraderie, safety, love, acceptance, respect) in people who are different from us (virtually everyone) is the result of competent personal diversity work. Creating environments in which everyone performs to full potential over long periods of time is the result of competent organizational diversity work. The combination of effective personal and organizational work produces healthy, high-performing people and organizations.

Implementating diversity work begins with the strategic allocation of resources to realize the stated goals. Actions are developmentally sequenced and based on adequate diagnoses. Personal diversity work is facilitated by professionals with good two-way communication, facilitation, group process, and instructional skills. Organizational work is also developmentally sequenced and conducted by people with change-management abilities. Data from periodic assessments, studies of best practices, and benchmarking results help guide the organization to a highly inclusive state. Attention to balance is continuous: Support is balanced with challenge. Recruitment and work on representation are balanced with work on retention and efforts to build a pluralistic climate.

In addition to knowledge and skills, leadership in diversity requires a mindset that values diversity. This frequently means being nonjudgmental and seeing something "different" as simply "not the same." Evaluation often must be suspended until sufficient knowledge has been acquired to achieve understanding. Because diversity work is not free of values, integrity and strong ethical principles are imperative.

Evaluating and Exchanging Feedback

Ongoing and periodic evaluations are needed to keep the initiative on an effective path. Evaluations are also useful for making proactive or responsive adjustments to changes in the environment. The full range of evaluation tools and techniques should be considered—qualitative and quantitative, formal and informal, perceptual and factual, analytical and intuitive, and observation and self-report—and evaluation should cover at least the following components:

- *Program evaluation.* Each discrete program (e.g., recruitment, mentoring, training, celebrations) deserves its own evaluations.

- *Representation.* People audits across levels and functions determine whether all appropriately measurable characteristics are distributed equitably and appropriately through the organization. While this may be comparable to an affirmative action audit, it should go beyond the categories typically addressed under affirmative action.

- *Climate.* Multiple data sources should be used to examine the organizational climate. The critical general question is whether the climate is different for specific individuals or members of specific groups. Both general organizational data and diversity-specific data should be studied.

- *Best practices and benchmarks.* Results of other evaluation work should be combined with studies of best practices in comparable organizations to evaluate diversity progress or status. More thorough benchmarking studies can be done to generate precise and quantitative comparisons.

- *External recognition.* Competing for external recognition can provide a structured look at how an organization is doing. An organization can strive to be known as a "best place to work" in general or as a best place for particular groups of people (e.g., mothers, women, gays and lesbians, African Americans, Hispanic Americans, international managers). External recognition gives diversity efforts a boost, and unsolicited honor has the greatest impact among internal members of the organization.

- *Overall organizational performance.* Examining the relationship between diversity progress and overall organizational performance is a powerful agent to sustain the case for diversity efforts. Results tend to be increasingly reliable and significant as the time period for analysis lengthens.

Chapter 7, The Road to Results, gives more detail on evaluation. Unless the organization is willing to act on the basis of ongoing evaluation data, it is generally not worth looking beyond what's known already. Effective organizations and professionals see that evaluation results are fed back to the organization and used to adjust its activities. This feedback must be packaged to be easily understood and used.

The evaluation task requires strong general research, evaluation research, and communication skills. Because the information obtained in evaluation is often sensitive, high standards of honesty, confidentiality, and integrity are essential.

Institutionalizing the Work

Competently led diversity work produces measurable positive outcomes. But proactive steps are needed to institutionalize the work accomplished in the key tasks we discussed above. Institutionalization has four basic ingredients:

1. *People resources.* The development and renewal of people to lead and do diversity work must become a core part of the organization's structure and processes. This means not just people designated to be responsible for diversity, but people in the organization at large.

2. *Diversity integration.* Diversity must be fully integrated with all major processes, practices, and policies. This includes both people-oriented and task-oriented matters.

3. *Education and training.* Every organization has turnover, and all employees need to continue their learning to renew prior knowledge and to learn new skills. Therefore, diversity education and training must continue—as an activity integrated with other development and as independent training as needed.

4. *Link to core functions and performance.* Making diversity an integral element in core functions of the organization reinforces its institutionalization. Linking it to overall organizational performance compels the organization to sustain the work.

In order to conduct the activities described above, diversity professionals need at least nine specific competencies.

NINE KEY DIVERSITY COMPETENCIES

- Leading head, hand, and heart work.
- Applying diversity-general and diversity-specific knowledge.
- Communicating effectively.
- Managing personal and organizational change.
- Conducting research.
- Exercising integrity and ethics.
- Managing stress.
- Establishing interpersonal relationships.
- Exhibiting critical personal attributes: a pluralistic mindset, openness, being nonjudgmental.

TEN SELF-EVALUATION AND INTERVIEW QUESTIONS

The 10 questions listed below provide a framework for self-review or for interviewing others. Acceptable answers are provided throughout this book. Key words for those answers are noted in parentheses after each question.

1. How do you define diversity?
   (inclusively; using words and experiences)
2. How do you gain support for diversity work from organizational leaders?
   (multifaceted compelling rationale; data; previously persuaded leaders)
3. How do you assess organizational needs?
   (multiple methods; several types of data)
4. Where do you start diversity education and training?
   (inclusive introduction first; specific issues later)
5. How do you design the education and training?
   (awareness through skills; developmentally sequenced; based on needs and issue identification)

6. Is there a role for human resource functions?
(eliminating barriers; integrating diversity into all
processes)
7. Is diversity relevant to functional or business systems?
(marketplace diversity; cross-functional team building)
8. How can this work be more cost effective?
(internal resource development; partnerships and
alliances)
9. What are advanced diversity work skills?
(issue-specific training; integrating diversity with quality;
incorporating diversity into functional planning)
10. What reduces resistance and prevents backlash?
(inclusive definition, address similarities as well as
differences; emphasize unity without uniformity;
developmental sequencing)

SUMMARY

- The five key concepts or elements with which diversity
  professionals must be familiar are developmental stages, a
  balance between support and challenge, organizational and
  systems work, personal work, diversity-general and
  diversity-specific work.
- Six key tasks for diversity professionals are gaining
  commitment, conducting diagnoses, designing
  interventions, implementing the work, evaluating and
  exchanging feedback, and institutionalizing the work.
- Effective and efficient diversity work requires professionals
  with competencies such as good communication,
  management, and research skills; integrity and ethics; and
  pluralistic, open, and non-judgmental attitudes.

Diversity Audit Process
A Sample Outline

Goal

Gather data needed by the organization to determine whether the existing work environment is conducive to recruitment and retention of a diverse workforce.

Objectives

Identify and develop a more thorough understanding of existing diversity-related issues and concerns, particularly those relating to race, gender, age, education, and language.

Provide the organization with essential qualitative data needed to:

- Determine next steps.
- Address high-priority issues and concerns.
- Engage in long-term planning and successfully shape future diversity-related activities.

The Process

1. Conduct one-on-one interviews and focus groups.
2. Identify key issues to be included in diversity survey.
3. Draft the survey.
4. Administer the survey.
5. Analyze the data.
6. Communicate results to team.
7. Identify subsequent action items.

Timing and Outcomes

Anticipated implementation: (Insert date)

Outcomes

1. Development of broad-based strategy and short-term tactical recommendations.
2. Management team consensus on key developmental areas and issues of highest priority.
3. Identification of next steps; formulation of a short-term action plan.

Participants

One-on-One Interviews

1. People of color: 5 representatives from each major group.
2. Summer 1995: 5 interns of color.
3. Leadership group: 4 representatives.

Focus Groups—Day 1

1. African-American exempt employees (8).
2. Other exempt people of color (10).
3. Exempt white males (random sample of 10).
4. Exempt white females (random sample of 10).

Focus Groups—Day 2

1. Managers and directors (10 representing various divisions).
2. Team leaders (7–8).
3. Nonexempt employees (random sample of 10).
4. New hires (random sample of 10).

Diversity Audit Schedule
Sample

Schedule	Tasks
Week 1	Conduct focus groups. Develop initial questionnaire. Review with management.
Week 2	Process organization review questions. Format questions in questionnaire layout. Management review of questionnaire mock-up.
Week 3	Process organization formats. Make revisions. Management approval of final questionnaire.
Week 3 or 4	Print questionnaires.
Weeks 4 and 5	Questionnaire deployment (2 week window to respond).
Week 6	Generate report.
Week 7	Brief management on report.

AFTERWORD

The authors continue to observe a growing worldwide need for diversity work:

In Sweden, one out of every 10 citizens was born in another country. In Germany, issues of religious and citizenship status are roots of violence. At any moment ethnic differences in the Balkans threaten to destroy a hard-won and uneasy truce. Throughout Africa, tribal conflicts continue with lethal results. In Japan and Korea, issues of race and gender difference continue to divide the population and compromise productivity. In Australia and all of the Americas, aboriginal peoples continue to be treated as second-class citizens.

Ignoring diversity can lead only to a dangerous future that marginalizes whole groups of contributors and excludes them from programs, communities, and society.

Diversity work contributes to the success of business and society by continuing to educate people, organizations, and communities to the benefits of heterogeneity and divergent thinking. Organizations with fewer diversity-related traumas and high levels of diversity-based synergy will be worldwide leaders in the global marketplace and community.

INDEX

Also available from McGraw-Hill Professional Publishing...

THE DIVERSITY TOOL KIT
Lee Gardenswartz and Anita Rowe

Any trainer can use this complete "program-in-a-box" to implement a thorough and effective diversity training program at any organization. *The Diversity Tool Kit* contains activity cards, sample agendas, skill-building exercises, questionnaires, and many other structured training tools that make it easy for managers—regardless of experience level—to organize effective, comprehensive training programs at a fraction of the cost of hiring outside trainers.
100 training tools (boxed set, 11" x 8½")   ISBN: 0-7863-0266-6 $300.00

THE DIVERSITY FACTOR
Capturing the Competitive Advantage of a Changing Workforce
Edited by Elsie Y. Cross and Margaret Blackburn White

In the face of a changing workforce, your organization must make cultural changes to remain competitive. *The Diversity Factor* is a compilation of essays that will help you develop new cultures and manage diversity successfully through education and awareness, strong leadership, and specific strategies that change outdated policies and practices. This book offers theoretical and practical information on how to deal with what can initially be a daunting issue.
284 pages   ISBN: 0-7863-0858-3 $35.00

IMPLEMENTING DIVERSITY
Marilyn Loden

In this practical and provocative guide, renowned diversity expert Marilyn Loden shares the strategies and tactics used by organizations truly committed to implementing diversity from the top down. 200 pages
ISBN: 0-7863-0460-X $20.00

Available at fine bookstores and libraries everywhere.